Women Who Shaped the World

Women Who Shaped the World

⊷

Renate Reiner

RESOURCE *Publications* · Eugene, Oregon

WOMEN WHO SHAPED THE WORLD

Resource Publications
An Imprint of Wipf and Stock Publishers
199 W. 8th Ave., Suite 3
Eugene, OR 97401

www.wipfandstock.com

PAPERBACK ISBN: 979-8-3852-3066-2
HARDCOVER ISBN: 979-8-3852-3067-9
EBOOK ISBN: 979-8-3852-3068-6

For more details see
https://www.esv.org/resources/esv-global-study-bible/copyright-page/

This is for Irene Graef, Carol Wenz, Faith Harold, and Shirley Russell, women who took upon themselves the task of mentoring a young, high school girl—recently converted and aimlessly wandering. They invested, taught, and molded me into a woman fit for vocational ministry. I am eternally grateful for their modeling of Titus 2:1–5.

Table of Contents

Preface

THIS BOOK ABOUT BIBLICAL women is neither complete nor exhaustive. It is, however, a sampling of biblical women who were chosen by God to perform specific tasks to teach us certain truths. We must learn from their example—their triumphs and defeats, their courage and vulnerability. They were instrumental in shaping our world and what they teach us has as much value today as when they lived it. We must understand this to learn from them and apply their lessons to our lives.

Acknowledgments

First, I thank God, my Savior, who enabled me to be a student and teacher of His Word. To my husband, Doug, who gently prodded and sometimes pushed me to the study of the Word and to teach what I had learned to people of all ages. I miss him every day. I thank my mother and aunt, Patty and Nancy, who believed the topic was viable and relevant.

Putting Things in Perspective

Then the Lord God said, "It is not good that the man should be alone; I will make him a helper fit for him."

Genesis 2:18

PERCEPTIONS THROUGHOUT HISTORY

OVER THE CENTURIES WOMEN'S roles and positions have been downgraded, maligned, and in many cases, reduced to that of a mere possession with no rights or merit in society. Many resources, both fiction and nonfiction, give insight into the world's perspective on women. How women were subsequently treated leads us to believe they had little to no value in the eyes of the public at large. This work is not meant to be another manifesto of how women need to stand up for themselves and fight the status quo. It is, however, an attempt to put the roles of women throughout biblical history in perspective.

There are many studies, historical writings, and a plethora of other sources to make my case, but that is not the purpose of this book. The purpose is for us to look at several biblical women whose lives made an impact on the shaping of history. They were defined by God's view of them in contrast to the world's view. They have much to teach us.

As with most false teachings, the world's perspective on women began with truth as God determined it. Over time, sinful

1

people began to question, cast doubt, and eventually distort God's truth to the point it became unrecognizable. The Lord gave Moses the Law and directed him to write the Pentateuch—the first five books of the Bible dealing with creation, the fall, and the establishment and explanation of the Law. Moses wrote it, but God gave him the words. It was God's purpose and perspective.

However, mankind is sinful. Our natures can't help but misinterpret and misrepresent the truth. Were it not for the Holy Spirit's leading, guiding, and illuminating, we would make a mess of the Bible and its interpretation. It has been this way since Adam and Eve committed the first sin in the Garden of Eden. We are all doomed to distort all the Lord had done.

By the time we get to Abraham's and Sarah's story, a shift in how women were perceived has taken place. While Abraham treated his wife, Sarah, with great honor and respect, the general perception of women's worth had been degraded. Some cultures even accused women of being the cause of all that was wrong in the world. All this happened before God carved the Ten Commandments on stone tablets and handed them to Moses to carry off the mountain.

The women at the time of the patriarchs had been relegated to their homes under the authority of their fathers, and later, their husbands. This aligns with Paul's charge to men and women in Titus 2:3–10. All women should pursue the characteristics mentioned in these verses. Older women should accept the role of mentor to the younger women. The responsibility of mentoring expands beyond other women and includes the importance of being a biblical influence on husbands and children as well.

As time moved forward from creation, women became vital in birthing and rearing children and serving the men in their lives, but nothing more. They were subjugated by their fathers and husbands, living under their authority, and considered to be inferior.

When we shift to the Greco-Roman culture prevalent during the time of Christ, we see that much had changed. Society then was similar to society today in that people tended to be free with their bodies and worship their deities. However, most women were kept at home caring for the household and out of politics. The problem? It was generally accepted that women did not have the intelligence or knowledge to form opinions or engage in stimulating conversations on political topics. It appeared they were only capable of having children and planning the feasts that were popular at the time. These parties could last for days. This systematic degradation continued well into the fourth and fifth centuries.

Even more disheartening was the fact that women were not allowed to own property. They couldn't own or operate businesses. They were refused the right to vote or hold political office. They were not encouraged to pursue degrees. The list goes on and on. Surprisingly, it took almost two millennia for women to push back and try to change the status quo held for centuries.

The Women's Suffrage Movement of the late 19th and early 20th centuries in the United States could very well have been the catalyst for the Feminist Movement that rose in the early 1970s. By 1920, women had won the right to vote and great changes began to take place. Women began to wear hemlines above the knees and haircuts in a short pixie style—a distinct contrast to trends just ten years earlier. Slowly, women began to enter the workplace and become part of the world outside their homes.

World War II forced women to take outside jobs to support their families because the men were away fighting a war. They became jacks of all trades, working assembly lines and starting their own businesses. They exchanged their skirts for more comfortable slacks, which served a dual purpose. Women had more freedom of movement and better leg protection while allowing them to climb stairs and ladders without exposing their undergarments to anyone on the ground. It was truly liberating but caused some family strife at war's end. The men came home fully expecting to pick up where they had left off, and women were reluctant to give up not just their jobs, but their independence as well.

Fast forward a few decades and women like Gloria Steinem and the ERA (Equal Rights Amendment) Movement came to the forefront inciting the female force to be militant about their rights. Today, the gender pay gap is eighty-four cents. This means that many women working full time will earn sixteen cents less per dollar than a man holding the same position. It wasn't the case in the 70s and early 80s when the gender pay gap was closer to sixty-four cents per dollar. My mother was an office manager at a large construction site and had many executive responsibilities. However, the men who held positions similar or equal to hers were receiving a higher salary. It was neither right nor fair, but it was the norm at the time.

The idea of feminism gained more traction when women began taking on roles that up to that time had been meant for men. Take the church for example. Women have been taking on pastoral positions more frequently in recent years. As a matter of fact, I drove by a Unitarian church recently that posted a banner welcoming their new pastor. There was a picture of a woman in clerical robes with a bright smile who was giving the peace sign. It definitely caught the attention of passersby.

As churches become more egalitarian in nature, they refuse to define the pastoral criteria. First Timothy 3:2–4 clearly states, "Therefore an overseer must be above reproach, the husband of one wife, sober-minded, self-controlled, respectable, hospitable, able to teach, not a drunkard, not violent but gentle, not quarrelsome, not a lover of money. He must manage his own household well, with all dignity keeping his children submissive." This leads to more and more chaos that bleeds outside of the church. The result is women putting their careers before their families and churches. The desire to climb the corporate ladder outweighs the desire to be an integral part of their children's early years which are crucial to teaching them a godly worldview and a healthy perspective on the family.

I'm not saying women should quit their jobs and stay at home with the kids. What I'm trying to say is that it's necessary to weigh the potential effect on the family during these years and the toll it may take. I'm the product of two full-time working parents. My brother and I had several hours to fill after school until they came home from work. We had chores to do and were expected to get our homework done. But when my parents came home, my mother made supper and we all sat at the table together and talked about the day's activities. My mother was home with us during our early years and my father always made it a point for us to do things as a family on the weekends and during the summer.

It's ok to have a full-time job. Just don't let it get in the way of what's truly important—your family. With that in mind, let's take a look at what the Bible says about the woman who juggles home and family successfully, all without damaging her relationship with the Lord. We're going to dive into Scripture and extract the truth as it relates to a biblical view of women by looking at the lives of several women in the Bible. Both Testaments encourage us to understand God's intent when He created Eve and called her a suitable helper. We'll also explore accounts during Jesus' earthly ministry and see how he broke down barriers of existing culture to demonstrate the proper way to treat a woman.

A Biblical View of Women

Her children rise up and call her blessed;
her husband also, and he praises her:

"Many women have done excellently,
but you surpass them all."

PROVERBS 31:28-29

WHAT THE BIBLE SAYS

GOD CREATED THE WORLD in seven literal, twenty-four-hour days. He prepared the world to sustain life and then created the life to occupy it. When he finished, he created Adam and gave him the task of maintaining the garden and caring for the wildlife. This account takes place in the first book of the Bible, Genesis. It's widely accepted that Moses wrote the first five books of the Bible called the Pentateuch. I will refer to Moses as the author in the following paragraphs.

In Genesis chapter 1 Moses gives the chronological account of creation. In Genesis 1:27 we read that male and female were created in God's image, but we don't read the account of Eve's creation until chapter 2. It seems Moses decided to take a step back and include her creation in a place where it could segue into the events that were to follow. In a sense, describing Eve's creation in chapter 2 gives it more meaning. As we think of all the events that took place on the sixth day of creation, we can't help but be in awe. Day six was packed with divine activity.

On day six the Lord breathed into existence all the wildlife except birds and fish, which were brought into being on day five. Then, God used the dust of the earth to form the man, Adam. God gave him the responsibility of caring for the plant life and wildlife. He also ordered Adam to give names to the animals, and as he did, it became clear there was not one that could be considered suitable for him to have a relationship with. Not a single creature of the animal kingdom was even capable of having a conversation with Adam. A relationship would not be possible without proper communication.

At this point, the Lord put Adam to sleep, took his rib, and made the woman. When Adam awoke, he saw Eve and, overcome with emotion, declares, "This at last is bone of my bones, and flesh of my flesh . . . " (Gen 2:23). They were two distinct humans made of the same material.

It is interesting though, that the first mention of woman's creation (Gen 1:27) is not of the process but the simple statement that she was created in God's image, just as man was. The Hebrew word for "man" (אָדָם / 'adham) in this verse is a generic term referring to the creation of human beings. Moses qualifies this later in the same verse stating they were created male and female. Moses first emphasizes that Eve was equally created in God's image as was Adam. The logical conclusion here is that women and men are equally created in God's image.

Exodus 20 relates the account of Moses receiving the law from God on Mount Sinai. The fifth commandment states, "Honor your father and mother" (v. 12). Since both parents were given the responsibility of rearing their children, it stands to reason they both should be esteemed. When we honor someone, we demonstrate their worth by obeying and respecting them. The Commandments are imperatives, not suggestions. We are to follow and apply them consistently throughout our lives.

If men and women were not considered equal in creation, they would not be considered equal in responsibility. This would then discard the necessity for children to obey both parents and the law would have referred only to the father as the one deserving honor. Parents, both male and female, are to be respected by their children. Neither is placed above the other in importance or honor.

Another truth women can claim is that they are equal in salvation. When Adam and Eve chose to sin by eating the fruit of the Tree of the Knowledge of Good and Evil, they knew immediately they had done something damaging and irreversible. How? They realized they were naked and tried to cover themselves with fig leaves. Later, when God was in the Garden, Adam and Eve hid themselves out of shame for what they had done. God called to Adam who responded with fear and embarrassment. God's next query, "'Who told you that you were naked? Have you eaten from the tree of which I commanded you not to eat?'" (Gen 3:11) The question was rhetorical and Adam's response was to blame Eve. It's interesting to note here that God directed his questions to Adam, not Eve. Adam, as head of the family, was held responsible even though Eve ate the fruit before he did. He chose not to stop her. The consequences were the same for all involved making all parties equal in condemnation.

The serpent, Satan, was made the lowest of the animal kingdom crawling on his belly. He also became enemies with the woman and her offspring. Eventually, the Savior, Jesus Christ would have victory over the curse.

Eve was cursed with bearing children in pain and focusing her desires on her husband who would be head of the home. Adam was cursed with hard labor and death, both physical and spiritual, being permanently separated from God. Physical death separates the body from the soul. Spiritual death separates the person from God. Death's curse also applied to the woman because she was equally guilty of sin. Adam and Eve had been created by God, lived and cared for the Garden, and they both chose to disobey God's explicit command to not eat the fruit.

So, why explain the particulars of the curse? The man, Adam, and the woman, Eve, were equally responsible for their sins and were punished accordingly. It's logical to conclude then, that they would have equal opportunity to be saved from that curse.

Fast forward several thousand years and we conclude that the Lord Jesus Christ shed his blood on the cross for all people. *All* people, not just one gender, one race, or one religion (1 John 2:2). Everyone has the same access to the salvation he so freely offers. What an awe-inspiring gift!

During the years of Jesus' earthly ministry and the beginning of the church age, some women were considered his disciples. Acts 9:36 specifically states Dorcas' status as a disciple. The women who accompanied Jesus on his journeys could be considered disciples. The word "disciple" wasn't reserved just for the twelve men Jesus chose and prepared for ministry. It describes any person who was a follower of Christ who actively believed the truths he was teaching. The Oxford English Dictionary defines the word "disciple" as: "a person who follows or attends upon another in order to learn from him or her."[1] There is no gender distinction in this definition. Anyone can be a disciple of Christ.

As well as being considered disciples, women were also vital to the establishment of the early church. Consider Dorcas again. She had an important ministry to the widows of Joppa. (Acts 9:36, 39) These women were often homeless and destitute with no means of income. Dorcas ministered to them by making clothing. The garments were precious to these women because they had no other option for obtaining new clothing when their old garments were in rags. We'll be discussing Dorcas later but suffice it to say she is an excellent example of the need for women in building the early church.

What Proverbs 31:10–31 Says:

> 10 An excellent wife who can find?
>   She is far more precious than jewels.
> 11 The heart of her husband trusts in her,
>   and he will have no lack of gain.
> 12 She does him good, and not harm,

---

1 Oxford English Dictionary

all the days of her life.

13 She seeks wool and flax,
and works with willing hands.

14 She is like the ships of the merchant;
she brings her food from afar.

15 She rises while it is yet night
and provides food for her household
and portions for her maidens.

16 She considers a field and buys it;
with the fruit of her hands she plants a vineyard.

17 She dresses herself with strength
and makes her arms strong.

18 She perceives that her merchandise is profitable.
Her lamp does not go out at night.

19 She puts her hands to the distaff,
and her hands hold the spindle.

20 She opens her hand to the poor
and reaches out her hands to the needy.

21 She is not afraid of snow for her household,
for all her household are clothed in scarlet.

22 She makes bed coverings for herself;
her clothing is fine linen and purple.

23 Her husband is known in the gates
when he sits among the elders of the land.

24 She makes linen garments and sells them;
she delivers sashes to the merchant.

25 Strength and dignity are her clothing,
and she laughs at the time to come.

26 She opens her mouth with wisdom,
and the teaching of kindness is on her tongue.

27 She looks well to the ways of her household
and does not eat the bread of idleness.

28 Her children rise up and call her blessed;
her husband also, and he praises her:

29 "Many women have done excellently,
but you surpass them all."

30 Charm is deceitful, and beauty is vain,
but a woman who fears the Lord is to be praised.

31 Give her of the fruit of her hands,
and let her works praise her in the gates.

My father-in-law was a great man of God, a man of vision, and a great missionary. He went to Brazil in 1948 to preach the gospel to people of a nation in darkness. During his early years, he faced severe opposition and persecution from other religious groups. He was also a man who loved a good joke and was quick to smile. He did have some opinions that I disagreed with, though.

In one conversation he was explaining to me why the executive committee, elected by the missionaries in the Brazil field to handle legal matters, consisted only of men. He said, "Sometimes we have to make difficult decisions so it's better for the men to be field leaders." I raised an eyebrow and with undeniable sarcasm replied, "Yeah, I have no idea how to make hard decisions." The women we will be studying in this book were clearly capable of making difficult choices and possessed other character traits that gave them the fortitude they needed to carry out the tasks they were given.

The virtuous woman of Proverbs chapter 31 makes a clear case for a woman's capabilities. She is a person to be modeled. The verses that reference all she accomplishes can be overwhelming, though. Reading the passage without considering context can lead us to believe the virtuous woman is capable of completing all the tasks in one day. I know me. I can be ambitious and I can be lazy. However I look at it though, I'm faced with the reality I could never do everything she does in one day.

After careful study of the text, I realized those accomplishments pointed to a greater truth. Everything she does is for the glory of God and the good of her family. There's no indication it is a list of daily tasks she checks off. Let's look at just a few examples.

The poet begins with the fact the excellent wife is valued far beyond any jewels because her husband has great regard for her. He trusts her to do good and not undermine his reputation. (Prov 31:10–12) It perfectly states how she respects her husband and how her heart is in the right place with the Lord.

This woman is industrious. (Prov 31:13–15, 24–25) She weaves fabric to clothe her family. and some of the garments are sold to provide income for the household. The clothing is used as a metaphor to describe her "strength and dignity." She is also up early to provide a meal so her husband and children are not hungry nor do they have to fend for themselves.

The virtuous woman handles business dealings skillfully. (Prov 31:16–19) She buys and sells property, works hard, and knows her product is of excellent quality. This speaks to her self-confidence in being able to handle complicated negotiations. People are much more likely to do business with someone who is confident in their capabilities and believes in their product. This woman is all that and more.

She is caring and compassionate. (Prov 31:20–22) God made women to be caring and nurturing by nature and we seem to adapt to the role of motherhood with ease. The virtuous woman's care and compassion extend beyond her own family as she reaches out to the poor and attempts to meet their needs. Her family is well taken care of with appropriate clothing and bedding that are made from the finest fabrics.

So, here is a big one. The virtuous woman does not embarrass her husband. (Prov 31:12, 23) I've had many conversations with women who are disgruntled with their spouses. The reason is usually mundane, such as, not putting his clothes in the hamper. A woman's complaints cast an unfavorable light on her man. It makes him look irresponsible and foolish. He may be all these things, but there is no good reason to malign him in front of others. It not only makes *him* look bad, but her as well.

That being said, I feel I need to clarify that the husband in this passage is a good man who cherishes his wife. He trusts her (Prov 31:11) and he praises her with, "'Many women have done excellently, but you surpass them all.'" (Prov 31:29) The paragraph above refers to a man like the Proverbs 31 husband.

It's pretty safe to say we've all had times we confided in a friend about our husband's quirks, bad habits, or annoying behavior. We may also have spoken privately with someone about problems between husbands and wives that affect the marriage. Sometimes couples may need to seek counseling in order to preserve their relationship.

But some women have husbands who are abusive. Domestic abuse takes several forms such as verbal, emotional, and physical. These are unhealthy relationships in which a woman can be in real danger. Women suffering from spousal abuse need to have the freedom to express their circumstances to those who can help them. They need to know someone will believe their cries for help and do something about their circumstances. Too many Christian churches and organizations "sweep things under the rug" so they don't have to deal with the situation or the abuser. As much as we would like to believe all marital relationships in the church are ideal, it's just not the case. We women should remember that the wife can exercise the role of the virtuous woman even though her husband doesn't reflect the qualities of the Proverbs 31 man. She is meeting her obligation before the Lord.

As we near the end of the list of her qualities we see the virtuous woman prioritizing her family for which they praise her. (Prov 31:26–29) The list of everything she does beginning in verse thirteen is for the good of her family. She prides herself in taking care of them. She also speaks highly of them. The result is her family praises her publicly. They consider her to be better than any other woman in the world. That is high praise indeed and not often heard today.

Lastly, and most importantly, the virtuous woman thinks in terms of eternity. She cares for her family. She cares for the poor. She handles business with integrity. She speaks well of her husband. She does all these things because they have eternal value. They are accomplishments she can place before the Lord and he will accept them as done for his glory. As she casts her crown at her Savior's feet, she will know she has done well.

As I read and reread this chapter, I am reminded of how much I have still to learn. The biblical women in this book reflect the truths we must apply to our own lives so we can be more like the virtuous woman and especially more like Christ.

DISCUSSION QUESTIONS

1. How have cultural changes throughout history influenced the roles of women in the local church?

2. How has feminist culture influenced the roles of women in history and in the local church?

3. How does the woman in Proverbs 31 counteract each of these thought bases?

PART 1

Women Who Birthed a Nation

Sarah - Mother of a Nation

*By faith Sarah herself received power to conceive, even
when she was past the age, since she considered him
faithful who had promised.*

HEBREWS 11:11

SARAH'S STORY

TO SAY SARAH'S LIFE was interesting would be an understatement.
Imagine being sixty-five years old in Ur of the Chaldeans and your
husband comes flying through the door, robes fluttering in his
wake, and says, "Honey, I've been talking with God and he wants
us to move."

Sarah's reply, "Move? Move where?"

"He didn't say," is Abraham's response.

"Wait! What now? How does he expect us to know where
to go? And don't you think we might be a little past our prime to
be packing up a house with a lifetime of memories to go . . . who
knows where?" Sarah responds with confusion written all over her
face.

Abraham is getting a wee bit irritated by now, which is evident in his rebuttal. "Sarah, God said he would *show* me where to
go. Let's get packed up."

Abraham and Sarah packed their belongings, loaded the
camels, and headed off to a place they had never seen. They most

likely left a home built of mud bricks packed together to form walls to live the life of nomads in tents. It could not have been easy for either of them—they were up in years—but they tackled the task and were on their way.

Ur of the Chaldeans was located at the extreme southeast corner of the fertile crescent in modern day Iraq. The city still exists today. Terah, Abraham's father, left Ur of the Chaldeans with Abraham, Sarah, and Lot, Abraham's nephew. The group traveled northwest to Haran where they stayed for some time. Terah died in Haran (Gen 11:31–32). At this point, God called Abraham to continue the journey to the land that he (God) would show him.

So, at seventy-five years of age, Abraham set out from Haran with his caravan containing livestock, servants, and many material possessions. Lot also joined them. The entourage was quite large, which would have made the journey slow going. Finally, they reached Canaan and God showed Abraham the land and declared that all of it would belong to his descendants. Abraham's response was to build an altar to the Lord and worship through the sacrifice of a lamb.

Famine forced Abraham to flee to Gerar (modern day Gaza) where he put Sarah in a precarious position by deceiving King Abimelech. During an audience with the regent, Abraham declared that Sarah was his sister. This prompted Abimelech to take Sarah into his harem. Abraham's desire to save his own skin was the cause of his deceit. The king could have had Abraham killed to have free access to Sarah. God appeared to Abimelech in a dream and told him his death was imminent because Sarah was, in fact, a married woman. God also closed all the wombs of the women in the king's house. Abimelech hadn't yet touched Sarah, which he attributed to the Lord keeping him from doing her harm. Nevertheless, as long as Sarah was in Abimelech's house, the women could not bear children. The king confronted Abraham the next day and returned Sarah to her husband.

Abraham lied to Abimelech by distorting the truth. Abraham and Sarah were half siblings. They had the same father (Gen 20:12). Abraham left out the fact she was also his wife. He also gave the excuse that he thought the Lord was not present in Gerar thus leaving Abraham exposed to danger. She would have been trapped in Gerar as a part of the king's household and harem. And all of this took place after God had made a covenant with Abraham that promised descendants more numerous that the stars in the sky.

Abraham and Sarah eventually returned to Canaan and parted ways with Lot. The elderly couple found a place to pitch their tents and settle in. They were both nearing their centennial year and still had no children. God had promised offspring, but time was marching merrily on; and Sarah was well into menopause. They had been waiting so long that Sarah was growing impatient, so she took matters into her own hands. She ordered Abraham to sleep with her Egyptian slave, Hagar. Abraham followed his wife's lead and slept with the slave girl who became pregnant.

Now things were getting really complicated. According to ancient custom, Hagar's child would be considered Sarah's. When Hagar realized she was pregnant, she became angry, causing her to look at her mistress with contempt. Hagar's contempt could be because she knew her child would become Sarah's. Most likely Hagar also felt used and violated. In fact, we could say she was raped by Abraham because she was an unwilling participant. As a slave with no rights, she was at the mercy of her mistress, Sarah.

Sarah became angry at this and blamed Abraham for her current suffering. She mistreated Hagar, causing the young slave to run away. The Lord met Hagar in the wilderness and told her to return to Sarah, because she would also be the mother of a nation.

When we read the account, we find Sarah's anger bewildering. After all, she gave Hagar to Abraham who followed his wife's lead. Abraham is not off the hook though. As head of the household and a man who feared the Lord, Abraham would have known God's promise of a son did not include Hagar. He should have refused Sarah's demand. He may have been trying to avoid conflict with his wife, but he should have remembered the covenant God made with him.

It's also confusing to understand why Sarah treated Hagar so harshly making it necessary for her to run. Perhaps Sarah was projecting her anger on to Hagar because she now had confirmation that their problem with infertility was hers and not Abraham's. I can only imagine how people going through the trial of infertility would understand Sarah's feelings. The way she went about bringing a child into the world doesn't justify her ill treatment of Hagar, but it causes us to be more compassionate toward Sarah. She had been waiting for the child God promised her for more than twenty years. In time, Ishmael was born to Hagar, but he was not the son God had promised to Abraham.

Eventually, God's messengers visited Abraham and announced Sarah's upcoming pregnancy and the birth of Isaac. Sarah was eavesdropping in the tent and laughed in disbelief. The visiting angels heard her laugh and chastised her with a question, "'Is anything too hard for the LORD?'" (Gen 18:14).

Twenty-five years had passed between the time God made his covenant with Abraham and Isaac's birth. The Lord opened Sarah's womb and fulfilled his promise using his own timetable. A year later, Isaac was in Sarah's arms and now she laughed for joy. At ninety years of age, Sarah gave birth to a son. She was not able to manipulate or alter the timeline or the circumstances. God's plan came to fruition and it was perfect.

THE CHALLENGES IN SARAH'S LIFE

As we contemplate Sarah's life, it's obvious that it had its challenges. She left a comfortable home to live the life of a nomad in a tent. Her possessions were constantly being packed and unpacked. She was forced to walk or ride a camel every time they moved to a new area. It could not have been easy for a woman of her age.

Sarah's life was subject to the direction of other people who were making decisions and plans without consulting her. Abraham told her they were going to a place God would show them and didn't ask her opinion or seek her counsel. When Abraham lied to Abimelech saying Sarah was his sister, she could have been raped. She wasn't given the respect or regard she deserved as Abraham's wife. In short, others were always managing her life.

As Sarah waited to have a child, she must have felt that God had abandoned her. It's easy to understand her impatience and the fact she attempted to take control in forcing Hagar onto Abraham. When we understand the cultural norms, that a woman's worth lay in her ability to bear children, we can recognize the rationale of her choice. A woman's main purpose as a wife was to give offspring, preferably male, to her husband. Women were under an incredible amount of pressure, and when they couldn't deliver, they were cast aside for another who would be more fertile.

We, of course, have the advantage today of reading the whole story and knowing its outcome. We can also be quick to judge Sarah for taking matters into her own hands. But when we think about how it must have felt being in such a crisis, not knowing what the future would bring we can have a different perspective and learn some valuable lessons. We'll see those in the next section.

THE LESSONS IN SARAH'S LIFE

I know from personal experience that God uses trials to give us an opportunity to grow. When my husband was diagnosed with pancreatic cancer in 2016, we were plunged into a year-long trial that would end with Doug's death and promotion to heaven. As hard as that year was, the Lord used that time to teach me some valuable lessons about facing the many fears I didn't realize I had. As we dealt with the chemotherapy aftermath by keeping trash-cans within arm's reach, we also saw the many opportunities to share our faith and respond to questions like, "How can you be so positive all the time?" I didn't always feel positive, but I was positive that God was and is in control at all times. We were never left on our own without hope.

I read in James, "Count it all joy . . . when you meet trials of various kinds . . ." (1:2–4). As I navigated each day and its trials, I could fully understand how such devastating circumstances could produce joy. My faith was tested and it was hard. It was the kind of test where you search the Word, pray and remember everything you have learned about God and his character. It was the kind of test where you come out the other end with your faith reinforced by the promises in the Bible. Today, there isn't any one thing I can think of which would cause me to doubt my faith. I am bolder about sharing it and defending it. I am more confident in it. I am more settled now than at any time in the past.

In the book of the Bible that bears his name, Job experienced a difficult trial of his own. Actually, to say it was "difficult" is a gross understatement. You could say he went through the wringer, was spit out the other end, then hung out to dry. I remember my grandmother and my mother-in-law describing their first washing machines. They washed and rinsed the clothes, but at the end of the cycle, the clothing had to be wrung out manually. There was a contraption attached to the tub that had two rollers mounted close together with a hand crank on the side. The clothing was fed between the rollers. The turning hand crank fed the garments through, essentially wringing the excess water out. The clothing suffered on its way through the wringer, spit out the other side, and hung out to dry. This was the nature of Job's testing.

Job's story can help us keep our own problems in perspective. No matter how hard our lives may be, Job's life reminds us of the deepest pain of unimaginable human loss and suffering. While it doesn't diminish the pain and suffering we are experiencing, we remind ourselves that we are not the only ones going through trials and focuses our attention off ourselves.

Probably the most valuable take-away from Job's experience is found in Job 23:8–10. He described searching for God in every direction and not finding him. Job felt abandoned. But even though it seemed God was distant, Job trusted that the Lord was still sovereign. He declared with conviction, "'But he knows the way that I take; when he has tried me, I shall come out as gold'" (Job 23:10). This is unwavering steadfast faith.

When our faith is firm and immovable, we can stand the fire of purification and become a person more useful to the Lord than ever before. This fire is the process used to refine precious metals, especially gold. The heat burns off impurities leaving the gold in its purest state, thus making it more valuable. Job's illustration is fitting for what he went through. Fire is used throughout the Bible to represent purification. Job had not sinned, but his faith needed to be refined.

With Sarah, we saw things went decidedly wrong when she tried to manipulate God's plan. Hagar was used and humiliated to the point of despising her mistress. Abraham was complicit in her plan. But it was probably Sarah who suffered most from her own mistakes. She was still without a child, her patience had run out, and her faith was being tested. So many times, patience and faith go hand in hand.

Those of us who are impatient can identify with Sarah. I am one of those people. I love fresh homemade bread, but I rarely make it from scratch. Waiting for the dough to rise high enough to make a decent slice for a sandwich, can get on my nerves. It seems to take forever while I check it every five minutes. I usually end up throwing the pan into the oven before the dough has fully risen, only to have a flat loaf when it's done. So, I got a bread machine. It was great! I just threw in all the ingredients, pushed a button, and walked away. A few hours later, voila! Hot fresh bread. I could slice off a nice chunk, slather butter all over it, and enjoy warm chewy bread any time I wanted. So much for learning patience.

If the Psalms had been written during Sarah's lifetime, they may have been helpful when trying to endure the waiting on God to carry out his plan. Psalm 27:14, "Wait for the LORD; be strong, and let your heart take courage; wait for the LORD!" She may have understood that waiting on God to move takes courage. Jumping in and trying to solve matters is the easy way out. Psalm 38:15, "But for you, O LORD, do I wait; it is you, O Lord my God, who will answer." Sarah would have realized God is sovereign and accomplishes his will in his time. Psalm 130:5, "I wait for the LORD, my soul waits, and in his word I hope." Sarah would have known to trust God's promises; that they will all be fulfilled in the end.

The one question I had during Doug's illness that was never answered was, "Why?" Why did the Lord do this at a time when we were making a transition from being on-field missionaries to Global Ministry Center personnel in Cleveland? Doug was fifty-two years old when he was diagnosed. He had already contributed so much to furthering the gospel in Brazil and we were looking forward to new opportunities to serve. I felt Doug still had so much to offer this world in his service to the Lord. God apparently thought differently, when a couple of months after turning fifty-three, Doug's race on earth was done. He had crossed the finish line. There are so many times I still wonder "Why?" Like Job, who never knew why he was subjected to his own season of trial, I've never received an answer.

After a while, I realized I was wasting my time asking for something the Lord may not answer to my satisfaction. I had forgotten that "No" is an answer. I was reminded in Isaiah 55:8, "For my thoughts are not your thoughts, neither are your ways my ways, declares the LORD." Then, Romans 11:33b states, "How unsearchable are his [God's] judgments and how inscrutable his ways." No matter how much I wished the Lord would do things differently, I understand I don't think like he does. I can only see a part of the picture. God sees the whole picture.

Sarah eventually birthed the child God had promised but took the long, winding path with pits and valleys along the way. When we realize God's thought process is different from ours and his that plan is specific, we can allow him to do his work. He does his work in us and in those around us.

Lest we think Sarah's life was one big failure, we need to highlight her victories. Because she did have them and they prompted New Testament writers to remind us of them. What Sarah may have been lacking in patience, she made up for in faith and faithfulness.

THE VICTORIES IN SARAH'S LIFE

As I think back on everything that happened to Sarah, whether by God's hand or her own, I see a steadfast faithfulness. When Abraham told her they were leaving for an unknown land, she packed up and joined him. Sarah went quietly along when her husband put her in danger of being violated in Gerar to avoid his own possible execution. And even though she forced Hagar on Abraham to bring about a child, Sarah remained faithful to her husband.

We can be sidetracked by the exhortation in 1 Peter 3:1-6.

> "Likewise, wives, be subject to your own husbands, so that even if some do not obey the word, they may be won without a word by the conduct of their wives, when they see your respectful and pure conduct. Do not let your adorning be external—the braiding of hair and the putting on of gold jewelry, or the clothing you wear—but let your adorning be the hidden person of the heart with the imperishable beauty of a gentle and quiet spirit, which in God's sight is very precious. For this is how the holy women who hoped in God used to adorn themselves, by submitting to their own husbands, as Sarah obeyed Abraham, calling him lord. And you are her children, if you do good and do not fear anything that is frightening."

The Genesis account of Sarah's struggle with infertility, impatience, and distrust of God's plan seems to be in complete opposition to what we read in 1 Peter 3:6. It calls us to follow Sarah's example of obedience, submission, and respect to her husband. We don't have every detail of every event in Sarah's life. We do have an example or two from which we can conclude her submission to Abraham. She left her comfortable life in Haran to spend the rest of it in a tent, and Sarah didn't contradict Abraham when they were before Abimelech. Those were the times she could have protested, publicly Abraham's authority. She did neither. She submitted to her husband's authority.

Submission to our husbands does not indicate we are weak and it certainly doesn't imply that wives are slaves. Submission starts with the wife, not the husband. A man can demand his wife be submissive as much as he wants. The wife is the one who resolves to submit to her husband's leadership. The woman who does this demonstrates spiritual maturity and the strength to set aside her pride.

The passage indicates we wrongly focus on the "external adorning" and disregard the "hidden person of the heart." We overlook the person who embodies this biblical attitude. Peter tells wives to be subject to their husbands in a manner that demonstrates Christ in their lives. Further, he encourages them because an unbelieving husband can be "won without a word . . . when they see [a wife's] respectful and pure conduct" (1 Peter 3:2). Sarah is labeled as a "holy woman who hoped in God" (1 Peter 3:5) because she demonstrated the person of her heart by obeying Abraham, "calling him lord" (1 Peter 3:6).

We all have doubts, weaknesses, and sins to overcome. None of us is perfect. However, we all have the opportunity to win the high praise of faithfulness from our husbands (Prov 31:10-31). Those of us without husbands will receive this praise from the Lord. We should all spend more time working on the hidden person of the heart rather than our outward appearance. I often tell young women to spend more time on their spiritual growth than on how they look as they leave the house.

As Sarah was faithful to Abraham, so she was to God. It was a natural outflow. Being true to a spouse demonstrates faithfulness to God because and the desire to glorify the Lord. Hebrews 11 mentions only two women in what's known as the Faith Hall of Fame—Sarah and Rahab. Hebrews 11:11 reminds us that Sarah believed in God's power declares Sarah received that "power to conceive, even when she was past the age." The Genesis account of Sarah's life gives us part of the story. We're told she laughed in disbelief when the messengers came to announce the birth of Isaac within a year. (Gen 18:12) After Isaac was born, she laughed for joy—joy the Lord had brought her even at her advanced age. (Gen 21:6) God performed a miracle in her body by reversing menopause.

Even though Sarah scoffed at the idea of her old, worn-out body being able to bear a child, the messenger's question, "Is anything too hard for the LORD?" (Gen 18:14) must have stopped her short. She must have recalled God's faithfulness during the last twenty-five years since he first called Abraham out of Ur of the Chaldeans. Sarah is listed among the faithful "since she considered him [God] faithful who had promised" (Heb 11:11).

We cannot fully understand Sarah's life and character by looking only at the narrative in Genesis. We get a decent, though incomplete, perspective on who she was. By looking at 1 Peter 2 and Hebrews 11, we learn the rest of the story and realize Sarah was not a failure. Far from it. She is an example of what it means to be both an independent woman and a submissive wife. The two can go hand in hand, but it is up to the woman to balance the two so her life glorifies the Lord. Sarah was that woman. She was a great woman of faith who was given the privilege of being the mother of a nation.

DISCUSSION QUESTIONS

1. Can you think of a time when you were tired of waiting for God to act and tried to handle problems yourself?

2. Can you think of a time you did wait on God and saw him work in a mighty way? Explain.

3. Can you think of a time when God called you to do something difficult? How can Sarah's example of obedience encourage us to do difficult things?

Rebekah - Playing Favorites

The woman was very beautiful, a virgin; no man had ever slept with her. She went down to the spring, filled her jar and came up again.

GENESIS 24:16

MY CHILDREN. OH, HOW I love them, but during the years they lived at home, both were notorious for accusing me of favoring one sibling over the other. If I did something, gave something or paid attention to one and not the other for any reason, my "error" was quickly pointed out. The truth, I realized one day, was that I loved, treated, and favored them equally. How did I know? They *both* accused me of playing favorites.

My little anecdote about my children might make you chuckle. Many parents could probably identify with me because it is just so hard to imagine loving one child more than another. I carried both my children and loved them unconditionally as soon as I knew I was expecting them. My son, the oldest, has always had a tender heart, his dad's intelligence and sense of humor. My daughter also takes after her dad in being aware of others' feelings, is diplomatic, and rarely offends anyone. Everyone who knows her loves her. She's also very intelligent. Both are uniquely different and equally loved and cherished by me because they are part of me.

Sadly, there are parents who favor one child and shun the other. A father may invest every ounce of energy into his son and rarely acknowledge his daughter. A mother may groom her daughter to either be just like her or be the person she always wanted to be while exercising little supervision over the other sibling. If we were to describe this family dynamic, we would certainly use the word "dysfunctional." We might even want to emphasize it by using all capital letters. The attitude of the parents and how they treat their children will reap consequences when they are grown. If parents are not being consistent in training or guiding those sons and daughters, the future results can be heartbreaking. As we delve into Rebekah's story, we will see several examples of this.

REBEKAH'S STORY - FAIRY TALE BECOMES DISAPPOINTMENT

When Sarah died, Abraham decided Isaac needed to marry. After all, he was forty years old and living at home. So, Abraham called his most trusted servant, Eliezer, to travel back to the area of Haran and find a wife among Abraham's people. It may seem odd to send a man on such a long journey since there were plenty of women in Canaan. Abraham was adamant. Isaac would have a wife of the same heritage, culture, and faith. The Canaanites were not known for their faith in God and many of those married to Canaanites were influenced to practice idolatry. Abraham didn't want that for his son.

Eliezer agreed to go. But being Abraham's servant, did Eliezer have a choice? Genesis 24:2–3 indicates he did. Abraham said, "'Please, put your hand under my thigh, and I will make you swear by the Lord, the God of heaven and the God of the earth.'" Eliezer then loaded up ten camels with supplies and gifts and started out for Nahor which may have been near Haran where Abraham sojourned until his father's death. Either way, the trip was long and arduous for the servant. Once Eliezer reached the city, he stopped outside the gates to rest by the town well and sought orientation from God. Eliezer prayed to the Lord and his request was very specific. He asked, "'Now let it be that the young woman to whom I say, 'Please let down your pitcher that I may drink,' and she says, 'Drink, and I will also give your camels a drink'—*let her be the one* You have appointed for Your servant Isaac.'" (Gen 24:14)

Lo and behold, as Eliezer looked up, Rebekah was coming to the well with her water jar. Every resident of the city retrieved water from the well for their personal use and to water their livestock. There was no central water supply in the city. Rebekah had a large jar on her shoulder to fetch water for the household. When she reached the well Eliezer asked for a drink of water which Rebekah quickly provided. Then she offered to water Eliezer's camels. God was answering his prayer exactly as Eliezer had asked.

As he watched in awe, Eliezer asked whose daughter she was. Rebekah's response confirmed she was the daughter of Bethuel, granddaughter of Nahor, Abraham's brother. Eliezer had found Abraham's niece. In his excitement, Eliezer told her he was sent by his master, Abraham, from Canaan to find a wife for Isaac. Rebekah ran and told her family all that occurred at the well.

REBEKAH'S CHARACTER

Now, let's turn our focus to Rebekah's character. Despite what we may think of her later in life, she demonstrated qualities that appealed to Eliezer.

Eliezer was standing near the well at evening when the young women came to draw water. The family had most likely used up the day's supply and would be needing more to last until the next morning. In the hot, dry climate, early morning and late afternoon into evening were the best times of day to go to the well because it was cooler than the middle of the day.

The jar Rebekah carried would have held about five gallons of water which she lifted onto her head or shoulder to carry home. Depending on the size of the cistern at home, she may have had to make several trips. The task required strength and endurance.

As Eliezer was finishing his prayer to the Lord, Rebekah arrived at the well. He asked for a drink of water which she gave him. Then she proceeded to water the ten camels that had made the trip without replenishing their water stores. After a journey such as the one Eliezer had made, the camels were each capable of drinking twenty to thirty gallons of water. Rebekah offered to water all ten of Eliezer's camels so she must have drawn at least 200 gallons with her five-gallon jar. It was no small task. As a matter of fact, it was hard work. Think about it. A five-gallon jar carries the amount of water in the jug of a modern water cooler. It's awkward and heavy. Rebekah must have made at least forty trips between the well and the water troughs.

It's clear from this incident that Rebekah was willing to serve without being asked and was an extremely hard worker. She was no delicate flower who sat at home doing nothing. She hauled water twice a day and engaged in all the other tasks expected of women at the time. She was neither lazy nor afraid to work.

The icing on the cake for Eliezer was learning Rebekah was a niece of Abraham. She was exactly the type of woman the patriarch wanted for his son, and she was exactly the person Eliezer asked the Lord to bring to him. Rebekah's brother, Laban, came out to meet the man. Eliezer told them the story of how he prayed for the Lord to show him the woman he had chosen for Isaac and how Rebekah immediately appeared. Eliezer also presented them with many gifts from Abraham to demonstrate the sincerity of his request. Rebekah received several pieces of valuable jewelry that day.

Normally, the negotiation for the bride and groom took place between representatives of each family. Eliezer's discussion with Rebekah's family ended up being somewhat irregular, though. Laban, as the family's spokesman, agreed to the marriage, but he wanted Rebekah to remain with them for another ten days. Eliezer was insistent that he begin his return journey immediately . . . with Rebekah.

Laban then said the decision was Rebekah's. Would she go with Eliezer immediately, or wait the ten days? She could decide if she was willing to make a long, exhausting trip to meet and marry a man she didn't know. Rebekah's decision demonstrated she was willing to accept radical changes to her life on short notice when she agreed to go with Eliezer. The young woman courageously prepared herself to face the unknown and journeyed back to Canaan with Eliezer. The next morning Eliezer, Rebekah and ten camels left for Canaan.

As they neared their destination, Isaac came out of his tent and looked into the distance. He saw Rebekah coming toward him with Eliezer. The young woman looked up at the same time, saw Isaac and asked Eliezer who the man was. When he told her it was Isaac, her groom, she covered her face with a veil and dismounted her camel. The action demonstrated her humility, modesty, and purity to Isaac. She was letting Isaac know she was able to be discreet and submissive to his leadership. She was also declaring she was a virgin. This was important to families of means because it would guarantee any children born during the marriage would belong to the husband and wife.

Isaac took Rebekah to the tent his mother, Sarah, had occupied before her death. He married Rebekah and loved her which comforted him. It's important to understand that Rebekah was a woman with moral convictions, a servant's heart, and a willingness to accept sudden changes. It's also pretty clear she was the woman God chose to continue the messianic line that began with Abraham.

REBEKAH'S ANGUISH

During a regular checkup when I was expecting my first child, the doctor commented the baby hadn't turned yet and was in a breach position. We weren't close to Alex's due date so the doctor said there was still time for him to turn. The baby was very active in the womb and gave me the impression he would be the child who never sits still. He is.

One day, Alex finally decided he needed to be upside down so he simply flipped himself over. I think I was standing in the kitchen when it happened and I just about flipped myself. It was so forceful and abrupt it knocked the wind out of me and I had to sit down. That's probably only a fraction of what Rebekah experienced.

Reading Genesis 24–26 tells us Rebekah's life was not all roses and butterflies. She came from a working-class family and was well acquainted with hard labor. However, when the "honeymoon" phase of her marriage passed, the problems started to manifest themselves. Like Sarah before her, Rebekah found herself dealing with infertility. It seems to be a recurring theme with the patriarchs, bringing distress to the women who suffered from it. Isaac and Rebekah waited twenty years for their twin sons.

When Rebekah finally conceived and those babies grew in her womb, the pregnancy became difficult and concerning. It seemed to her the babies were with wrestling each other, something boys often do, only outside the womb. The constant movement and agitation made her uncomfortable. She asked the Lord to give her an idea of what was happening. His answer was, "Two nations are in your womb, and two peoples from within you shall be divided; the one shall be stronger than the other, the older shall serve the younger." (Gen 25:23) I can only imagine what Rebekah thought of that response from God.

The theme of a younger child taking precedent over the oldest appears time and again throughout Scripture. Isaac, Jacob, Joseph, Judah and David were all younger than their oldest siblings and they were the ones God used to perpetuate the messianic line. I'm not sure why that is, but my best guess would point to Jesus. He had to be the first. He was firstborn to a virgin, he was first to ride an untrained donkey into Jerusalem, and he was first to be buried in the tomb Joseph of Arimathea bought. Everyone that came before were chosen for varying reasons. Messiah was first.

The fulfillment of the Lord's statement came when the twins were born. Esau came first with Jacob literally holding his brother's ankle. They were very obviously fraternal twins. Esau was covered in red hair and resembled a Viking ready for battle. Jacob was smooth skinned with a different hair color. As the boys grew, it became obvious Isaac preferred Esau who was an outdoorsman and loved hunting. Rebekah favored Jacob because he was a homebody preferring to stick around the tents occupying himself with more domestic pursuits.

The rivalry between the brothers is evidenced in the account of Jacob manipulating the right of the firstborn from Esau over a bowl of lentil stew. (Gen 25:29–34) Esau was famished and Jacob essentially talked him out of the inheritance reserved for the first-born by withholding the stew until Esau agreed to Jacob's terms.

Later, a famine in the land of Canaan forced the family to migrate to Gerar. Does this remind you of Sarah? Isaac, being his father's son, lied to the Philistine king, Abimelech, about his relationship with Rebekah. In Sarah's story we saw that Abraham deceived Abimelech. The term "Abimelech" was a title given to the leader of the Philistines so the king whom Isaac deceived was a different person. Isaac's encounter was also many years after Abraham's.

When Isaac was questioned about Rebekah, he told the king she was his sister which was an outright lie. This exposed her to the possibility of sexual abuse, just like her mother-in-law before her, at the hands of the Philistines. Rebekah could very well have become a concubine in Abimelech's harem. Rebekah was a beautiful woman and would have turned the heads of many men. It was also common in that culture for an unattached woman to be taken and forced into a harem.

It appears Isaac was not looking to Rebekah's best interest. He was more concerned with his own life. Isaac may have thought it would be worse for him to die than it would be for Rebekah to endure repeated rape. He probably didn't realize there are fates worse than death. He was motivated by self-preservation. When the king saw Isaac showing affection to Rebekah, he confronted Isaac who confessed Rebekah was, indeed, his wife. Abimelech kicked them out of his country. Yes, it sounds like a rerun.

REBEKAH'S FAULTS

When it comes to character flaws, as with all of us, Rebekah had several. We know she favored Jacob, who had a milder disposition than his brother, Esau. Rebekah spent more time with Jacob which gave her a certain manipulative power over her son. Isaac invested in the older son, Esau. It may be that Isaac would have naturally paid more attention to the eldest because, by law, Esau would be his heir. Normally, the one destined to take over the estate when the patriarch is gone is often treated and educated differently. He is groomed to be adequately ready to assume the position of head of the family. But Esau had sold his right to inherit over a bowl of stew making his disregard for tradition obvious. Jacob, on the other hand, understood the significance of being primary heir and it is probably the reason he went along with Rebekah's machinations.

Isaac was on his deathbed and ready to bestow the family blessing on his eldest. By this time, he was feeble, blind, and bed bound. Isaac called Esau and sent him out to hunt game and make his favorite stew. While Esau was gone, Rebekah contrived a plan to trick Isaac into giving the blessing of the firstborn to Jacob.

She and Jacob made a stew and flavored it the way Isaac liked it. Rebekah covered Jacob with animal skins to give the impression he was Esau and sent him into Isaac's tent. The disguise served two purposes. When Isaac felt the hair on Jacob's arms and smelled the odor of the animal, he would think it was Esau. Jacob didn't have hairy arms, nor did he smell like game. Jacob went into the tent with the stew and lied to his father about who he was. Isaac was confused because he heard Jacob's voice, not Esau's. Jacob insisted he was Esau so Isaac asked him to come closer. After feeling and smelling Jacob, Isaac was satisfied and gave his younger son the blessing. Then Jacob walked out of the tent. When Esau returned from the hunt and learned what had happened, he pleaded with his father to give him a blessing too. But Isaac was permitted to give only one. Esau's fate was sealed.

Then, using a manipulation tactic with Isaac, Rebekah announced her distaste for the two Hittite women Esau had married.

Canaanite women did not have the spiritual or moral beliefs the women from Rebekah's family would have. She over dramatized how useless her life would be if Jacob married one of the local Hittite women prompting Isaac to send Jacob away to Padan-aram (vicinity of Haran) to marry one of Laban's daughters. Remember, Laban was Rebekah's brother.

Jacob was also sent away after gaining his father's blessing because Esau had vowed to kill his brother for usurping what he felt he was entitled to. Jacob left for Padan-aram and would spend forty years there before going back to Canaan.

By the time Jacob returned many years later, Rebekah had died. She had sent her favorite son away and never saw him on this earth again. God had said the younger brother would be greater than the older. Rebekah favored Jacob over Esau and tried to manipulate events to bring about the result God had predicted when she was pregnant. All it did was cause conflict within the family that wouldn't be resolved for forty years. It's a troubling ending to a sad story.

Rebekah's interference wasn't necessary. God's promises are always fulfilled and he will make them happen one way or another. God uses us best within the parameters of his will. The problems start when we insert ourselves in an attempt to take control. Usually, it doesn't end well for us.

Many events in our lives can be uncomfortable, distressing, and unbearable at times. My husband's illness was all of those. Both of my children supported decisions Doug and I made about his treatment. We were unified. But I was often trying to convince doctors of taking a direction I thought was best. I met with plenty of resistance because God's sovereignty, his loving control, was impeding the way. In my desperation, I was allowing my circumstances to dictate my actions and it was the wrong approach. It is also a lesson Rebekah must have learned.

We've all had those moments when we realize our circumstances shouldn't be our primary focus. God should. Why is that? Because our actions will rarely change the events. We all suffer and we all want certain things for our lives. We can try to manipulate events to produce the outcome we want, but in the end, God is always sovereign and does his will his way.

DISCUSSION QUESTIONS

1. What do you think Rebekah's initial thoughts were when Eliezer showed up with a proposal and gifts?

2. In what ways did we see history repeat itself in Rebekah's story?

3. What is the greatest lesson we can learn from Rebekah's life and how does it apply to you specifically?

PART 2

Women of a Chosen People

Miriam - Finishing Well

Then Miriam the prophet, Aaron's sister, took a timbrel
in her hand, and all the women followed her, with
timbrels and dancing.

EXODUS 15:20

MY FATHER-IN-LAW, HAROLD REINER, was a great missionary and he was active in Brazil for 60 years. He had a love for people and a gift for preaching the Word so others could understand. This was a crucial gift for one working with largely illiterate people. Harold Reiner was known as a man of great wisdom. The room hushed when he got up to speak.

During his years of service, he and his wife, Joan, established several churches in Northeast Brazil. Harold's stark white hair made him easily recognizable and people called out to him everywhere he went. The fact the white-haired missionary also flew an airplane elevated him to celebrity status.

The last church Harold established had been nationalized for many years and he and Joan attended the meetings more and served less. The younger generation was maturing and gradually assuming responsibilities in the church. They also had some new ideas on evangelism, music, dress, etc.

I've discovered that as we age, we become less tolerant of change and Harold was no exception. he would often stand up in business meetings and start talking, then he would go off topic, thus extending the meeting well beyond lunch time. And what he had to say wasn't particularly relevant. Sometimes it was even a little inappropriate. It was a desperate attempt to remain relevant which did more damage than good. It was almost as if he was throwing away all the effort and wisdom, he had needed to get the church going. He wasn't content to let the younger people bring in music they thought was more compatible or insert himself in the decisions the leadership of the church made. He couldn't be content and watch them lead without making a comment. He was on a dangerous path to "not finish well."

Hebrews 12:1–2 states, "Therefore, since we are surrounded by so great a cloud of witnesses, let us also lay aside every weight, and sin which clings so closely, and let us run with endurance the race that is set before us, looking to Jesus, the founder and perfecter of our faith, who for the joy that was set before him endured the cross, despising the shame, and is seated at the right hand of the throne of God." Think about the context in which we find these verses.

The previous chapter, 11, listed a number of biblical figures who were known for their faith. Those listed are mostly men, but there are two women—Sarah and Rahab. These two demonstrated unwavering trust in God believing he would fulfill his promises. All of those listed in Hebrews 11 are the cloud of witnesses in the first verse of chapter 12. These are the ones who finished well.

Now, let's look at the parable of the talents in Matthew 25:14-30. Jesus told a story about investing talents (a form of money) while the master went on a long journey. This wealthy man called in three servants to entrust each of them with a sum of money while he was gone because it would be a while before he returned. He gave each man an amount within the servant's capacity to manage. The master expected results based on what he knew of each servant. To one servant he gave five talents, to the next he gave two talents, and one to the last servant. Then, he went on his way.

When the master finally returned, he summoned those servants to receive his money in return plus whatever interest it may have accumulated. The first servant approached and gave his master the original five talents and five more he had earned in interest. When the second servant handed over his money, it had also doubled in value. What had been two was now four. Now, the third servant came forward and, instead of handing over the coin, he gave an excuse. The servant stated how he knew the master was a hard man and that he received return even from places he didn't invest. So, the servant took the one talent and hid it.

The master turned to the first two servants and called them "good and faithful." The third he called "wicked and slothful." The servant was then instructed to give his one talent to the servant with ten and was unceremoniously cast into the outer darkness. There was no coming back from the consequences of that lesson.

The parable teaches us several lessons. First, God gives us the tools we need to carry out the mandate to share our faith and evangelize. (Matt 28:19–20) Second, he expects believers to be serious about investing their lives to tell others what Jesus accomplished on the cross for them. Third, believers will give an account to the Lord and return to him what was entrusted to them. Finally, those who choose not to share the gospel with unbelievers and hide their Christianity, should examine their own lives to determine if they are truly converted and redeemed by the blood of Jesus Christ. It's about following through and finishing well.

So how does this relate to Miriam? It's a logical question. Let's focus on the third teaching point, the fact we are all accountable to the Lord. The end of the parable emphasizes the faithfulness of two of the servants. The third servant didn't follow through on his obligation and received severe punishment as a result. Christians, we must remember that our obligation to share the gospel with others is a lifetime commitment. It's a task we will carry to the grave and we need to persevere. In this context, finishing our lives well means dying with our boots on. We don't get vacation. We don't get sick days. We don't retire. With this principle in mind, let's see the high and low points of Miriam's life and what we can learn from them.

MIRIAM'S STORY

The curtain opens on a scene in the land of Egypt. The children of Israel have been in this country for 400 years. The life they enjoyed when Joseph brought his family down is all but forgotten. The Hebrews are now slaves to the Egyptians and are enduring a life made miserably difficult because of the back breaking labor required of them.

Making bricks in any context requires physical strength and attention to detail. The form is heavy and must be turned over to release the newly made block. If the water to sand and cement ratio is not correct, the brick will crumble when it's turned out. On top of that, the Hebrews had a daily quota to fill which could provoke severe beatings if not met. The task masters were ruthless in handing out punishment and the people were groaning under the burden.

This is the context for Miriam's early life. She was the oldest of three children. Her younger brothers were Aaron, three years old, and Moses, a newborn. Add to that the paranoia of a pharaoh who feared being overrun by the Israelites because of their number and we have a recipe for persecution and genocide.

Pharaoh issued a decree that all male Hebrew children under the age of three were to be slaughtered thinking the numbers of the Israelites would be curbed. The Hebrew midwives were also ordered to kill the newly born male children. These women refused to obey the law knowing God would not be pleased if they did. They skirted the issue by declaring to Pharaoh that the Hebrew women were so robust they would give birth before the midwives arrived. This act of defiance saved many young boys' lives. It will be interesting to meet the midwife who spared Moses' life when he was born. She most likely had no idea of the impact this would have on world history.

Moses was born to Amram and Jochebed who hid him for three months. As the baby boy grew it became harder and harder to keep him hidden from prying Egyptian eyes. Jochebed wove a basket out of papyrus reeds and covered it with pitch so it would float. Then she carefully laid Moses in the basket and put it in the Nile River. This seems dangerous on several levels, but it demonstrates Jochebed's desperation. She took so much care in weaving the basket and waterproofing it. Then she placed the baby in the basket and set it to float down the Nile where hippos and crocodiles were constantly on the lookout for fresh food. Moses' chances of survival were pretty slim—except God was moving.

Jochebed put Miriam in charge of watching to see what would happen to the baby. It may have been to bring Moses back home if no one picked him up. It may have been for other reasons. No matter. Pharaoh's daughter came down to the river to bathe and spied the basket in the rushes. She ordered one of her maids to retrieve it and discovered the obviously circumcised baby boy. Pharaoh's daughter decided to adopt him as her own child and named him Moses because she "drew him out of the water."

The princess had one dilemma. She had no means to feed the baby as he was still very young and would need mother's milk. It was at this point Miriam appeared with a solution. She told the princess she knew a woman who would be able to nurse Moses until he was weaned. Pharaoh's daughter readily agreed and Moses went back home to his family safe and now protected. Moses was no longer in danger of being killed and he would spend the next three or so years with his family. God's handling of the matter was awe inspiring and ironic at the same time.

What does this little narrative tell us of Miriam, though? We know her life and that of all the Hebrews was extremely difficult. They suffered great oppression and lived in constant fear of their lives. The children of Israel were subject to almost unbearable slave labor that benefitted only the Egyptians. And the Israelites faced possible extinction because of Pharaoh's edict to slaughter all male children under three years of age.

One thing we can surmise from the text in Exodus 2 and later in the New Testament (Heb 11:23) is that Miriam's parents feared the Lord more than they feared man. They sought a way to save Moses' life not knowing what the outcome would be. When Jochebed placed Moses in the basket she had no notion of how great a figure he would become. All she cared about was saving her baby. And Jochebed did this because she knew God's mercy and grace far outweighed Pharaoh's paranoia and wrath.

Miriam was an obedient and responsible daughter. We don't know how much older she was than Moses, but we can be sure she was old enough to be able to follow the basket down the river, observe Pharaoh's daughter pulling it out of the Nile and come up with a plan to bring Moses back home to his family. This indicates she was also very intelligent, something that would prove itself again as she assisted her brothers in leading the children of Israel out of Egypt and slavery.

MIRIAM'S SERVICE

The time had finally come for the children of Israel to leave Egypt. They had seen nine plagues ravage the land and Egyptian people. Several times Pharaoh had said he would release the slaves only to renege and order them to get back to work making bricks. For the most part, the Israelites had been untouched by the plagues. However, the tenth plague would be different. That plague could affect the Hebrews as well as the Egyptians if they didn't follow God's instructions exactly.

Moses told the people to prepare for the Passover. They were to kill their perfect lambs and paint the door posts and lintels with the blood. Special instructions followed on how to prepare and eat the meal as well as how they should be dressed. The people were to be ready to go at a moment's notice because the window of opportunity for escape would be small.

The angel of death came through and killed the first born of every person and livestock not protected by the blood of the lamb. When the angel arrived at a house with door posts and lintels covered in lamb's blood, he passed over it and no death came to it. Pharaoh's palace was not protected with the lamb's blood. As a result, he lost his first-born son and, in his grief, ordered the Hebrews out of the land. Moses wasted no time. The Israelites were ready. The people of God marched hastily out of Egypt.

It didn't take long for Pharaoh to regret his decision to let the children of Israel go. He gathered his army and took off after them and caught up with them at the Red Sea. The Israelites, having just reached the safety of the other side, looked on terrified as the Egyptian army entered the seabed while the waters were still parted. Pharaoh's decision to follow would prove his undoing. He raced after the Hebrews along with his army and, as they reached the middle, they were swallowed up by the water returning to the seabed and drowning every last one. I imagine people watched with horror and relief. They watched in horror as the Egyptians drowned. They watched in relief because they knew they were truly free.

Miriam, overjoyed, gathered the women to lead a song of worship to the Lord. She grabbed her tambourine and went out dancing and singing, "Sing to the LORD, for he has triumphed gloriously; the horse and his rider he has thrown into the sea." (Ex 15:21)

Miriam was not just a leader, but one who had the respect of the people. Not just anyone can grab and instrument and incite women to follow her in worship to the Lord. She didn't have to go gather the women and convince them to join her in song. She took up the tambourine and the women followed. In general, people will only follow someone they respect.

Hundreds of years later, when the nation of Israel had turned its back on the Lord, the prophet Micah reminded the people of what God had done. "For I brought you out of the land of Egypt and redeemed you from the house of slavery, and I sent before you Moses, Aaron and Miriam." (Micah 6:4) It's significant that Micah felt the need to include Miriam's name in that text. It acknowledges her leadership along with Moses' and Aaron's. She played an important role in freeing the slaves—a role that began way back when she followed a basket down the river and devised a way for Moses to survive.

Not only was Miriam a woman well respected for her leadership skills, but she also left a legacy of leadership for women and men alike. Normally, when we read through a biblical genealogy, only the men are listed from generation to generation. Levi's descendants are listed in 1 Chronicles 6. The third generation from Levi lists Amram as the firstborn son of Kohath. Amram's children are listed in verse three. They are Aaron, Moses and Miriam. Miriam is the only woman who appears in the genealogy. It's an odd occurrence and we can only speculate as to why her name is there because God doesn't always explain his motives. However, to be listed in a genealogy of the priestly line of the nation of Israel is significant.

God would not have allowed her name to be added had Miriam not been a woman of faith and fortitude. She followed through on her task to keep an eye on her brother as he drifted down the Nile. She burst out in a song of praise after crossing the Red Sea and escaping Pharaoh. She left a legacy worthy of being mentioned in a list of names hundreds of years later. We can even conclude Miriam was a near perfect woman. She was not.

MIRIAM'S SHAME

Numbers 12 begins with Miriam and Aaron complaining about the Cushite woman Moses married. They questioned Moses' integrity and position as prophet and leader of the people of God. The Lord, of course, heard their complaint and decided he needed to have a little chat with the three siblings at the tent of meeting. It must have been similar to being called to the principal's office in school. One never knew quite what to expect. They just knew they were in trouble.

The Lord reminded all three that he had chosen Moses because he was meek, humble and faithful. God explained himself to Aaron and Miriam, but he didn't need to. He had chosen Moses to be his special messenger to Pharaoh and the Israelites. Quite frankly, God was merciful in his explanation.

God was also angry that the topic had even come up, and as punishment, he struck Miriam with leprosy. Aaron and Moses were quick to rush to her defense even asking the Lord to pass her punishment to them. They were willing to suffer the consequences of Miriam's sin which would have been banishment from the camp. Leprosy was a highly contagious disease that slowly ate the body's flesh leaving gaping wounds and loss of extremities. It was devastating and a person with leprosy was ostracized and isolated.

God healed Miriam within moments of becoming leprous and restored her. She was still unclean, though, and had to spend seven days outside the camp, the length of time designated to verify the disease was gone. Because Miriam was so highly respected, the people would not leave that spot until she was brought back into the camp.

Miriam was struggling. She was loved and respected, but she must have also fought feelings of pride and resentment. She worked just as hard as her brothers in leading the people, yet Moses got all the credit and Aaron was appointed high priest. She probably saw herself as irrelevant and useless which is a common feeling for those who have spent a lifetime in ministry.

As we age and slow down it's difficult to accept there are tasks better left for the younger generation. Taking on a large children's Bible class by myself would not be wise on my part at my stage in life. It's prudent for me to have several helpers who can do things like getting down on the floor to pick up crayons. But as a person who has invested her entire life in the gospel ministry, I'm sometimes frustrated to discover I'm not able to do those great things anymore. We reach our fifties and realize we can't do what we did while in our twenties. Our joints don't move as freely. It takes a little longer to get in and out of the chair. Soon, the younger generation is taking over the responsibilities we once held, and they appear to do it without any effort. It's discouraging. But we have an obligation to finish well.

We must always keep in mind the task God has given us on this earth. We are to go, preach and make disciples and we are to do it faithfully. When the next generation comes along, we can now become mentors and encouragers. This doesn't make us irrelevant. It gives us a unique opportunity to minister in a manner we hadn't been able to before. It's important that we obey the Great Commission, persevere, and embrace the new opportunities we are given instead of wishing for what we can't have or trying to keep doing the things we always have. It's time to let the younger ones take over. There are always opportunities to serve in other capacities.

Miriam was most likely upset over the fact she hadn't been chosen as one of the seventy elders to assist Moses in his day-to-day decision making. (Numbers 11:16–23) Not being selected did not imply she wasn't qualified. It was hard to accept being passed over for another, but her lack of a gracious spirit put a bit of a damper on the accomplishments of the past. Miriam would never be truly irrelevant. Her ministry could have evolved differently. She needed to keep going in another capacity.

As we journey through this life, as difficult as it may be, it's important to keep in mind that what we do now is great, but it's not everything. New opportunities for service to the Lord will present themselves and when they do, we should be ready. This attitude indicates our desire to continue until we're called home so we can hear him say, "'Well done, good and faithful servant.'" (Matt 25:23) That's a life well-lived.

DISCUSSION QUESTIONS

1. Think - What is your "Achilles Heel"? What is the one thing that could possibly lead you to undo all the good you have done for the Lord so far?

2. What measures can you take to prevent this from happening?

Rahab - Courage under Fire

By faith the prostitute Rahab, because she welcomed the
spies, was not killed with those who were disobedient.

HEBREWS 11:31

THE CHILDREN OF ISRAEL were poised to take over the Promised
Land. The Israelites had been wandering in the desert for forty
years and were excited to enter the territory God had promised to
the Hebrews since the time of Abraham. The generation of people
who had doubted Joshua and Caleb's report of abundance and
prosperity after scouting out the land were dead. Only those who
were born during the desert wanderings along with Joshua and
Caleb would be allowed to enter this land "flowing with milk and
honey." Joshua, the newly appointed leader of the nation needed
information about what they might face on the other side of the
Jordan River. He chose two men to go to the city of Jericho on a
reconnaissance mission.

The two spies crossed the river and snuck into Jericho. As
they wandered the city, they scouted out information about its
defenses and the people's attitude toward the Hebrews. When they
tried to sneak back out of the city, the king's guards learned of their
presence. The spies attempted to flee and ended up pounding on
the door of Rahab's inn. This woman was well-known as the town
prostitute and her "inn" may very well have been a brothel. The
text doesn't say whether it was a house of prostitution, nor whether

the spies knew this fact. One thing was certain, knocking on a prostitute's door would guarantee entry. Once they were inside, they began a conversation that would have a profound influence on the future of the royal line of Israel.

The king's guard arrived at Rahab's door in their search of the spies. She told them the spies had been there but had already left to rejoin their camp. The truth was the spies were still in the house. As a matter of fact, they were on the roof hiding under stalks of flax. As soon as she closed the door on the king's guard, Rahab ran up to the rooftop. What followed is a beautiful declaration of faith in the Lord of the Hebrews. (Joshua 2:9–13) Rahab then asked the two men to spare her life when they returned to conquer Jericho. The spies took an oath and promised that she and any people in her house would not die at the hands of the Israelites. In order for the Hebrews to know which house not to destroy, she must hang a red cord or rope out the window. Rahab's house was situated on the city's wall so she put the scarlet cord out the window after the spies had left. It would be clearly visible on the outer wall giving the location of Rahab's family. Because she held up her end of the agreement by hanging the scarlet cord, the Israelites held up theirs. Rahab and her entire family survived the invasion of Jericho.

The scarlet cord symbolizes Rahab's faith and the theme of the scarlet thread is seen in other biblical texts. For example, take the twins, Zerah and Perez, born to Judah and Tamar. Zerah's arm came out of the birth canal and the midwife put a red ribbon on it saying he was the firstborn. However, Perez was actually the first one out of the womb. (Gen 38:27–30) Scarlet thread was used to sew the curtains of the Tabernacle together. (Ex 26:1) These examples of scarlet, the color of blood, are pictures of the blood that flowed from the body of Christ when he hung on the cross hundreds of years later. They foreshadowed the coming sacrifice of our Savior.

The culmination of the narrative of Rahab and the conquest of Jericho is that the city fell after the Israelites had marched around it for seven days. Rahab became part of the nation of Israel when she married an Israelite and had a son named Boaz. Yes, the Boaz from the book of Ruth whom we will study in a coming chapter. If we follow the lineage of David, second king of Israel backward, from Boaz to David, we discover Rahab was David's great-great-grandmother. What we learn is that God can use any person in any situation for his own honor and glory. Rahab's character played a part in this.

RAHAB'S CHARACTER

Rahab was an industrious woman and did not shy away from work. She owned the inn where the two spies hid from the king's guard. We can conclude this from the language used in Joshua 2:1. The ESV (English Standard Version), NIV (New International Version), and the NKJV (New King James Version) all say, "They came to the house of a prostitute." The wording indicates Rahab's ownership of the property rather than her being an inhabitant. She took the initiative to hide the spies and to speak with the guard. She assumed all responsibility for everything that happened in her home.

Joshua 2:6 leads us to believe she may have been a weaver of fabric or a seamstress. Rahab took the spies to her rooftop and told them to hide under the stalks of flax that had been laid out to dry. When flax was harvested it was soaked in water for four weeks in order to break down the fibers. The fibers were separated and spread out carefully in rows to dry on the rooftop of the house They could cover the entire roof in several layers. Once the fibers were completely dry, they could be woven into fine linen and used to make clothing.

The process required hard work and attention to detail. Linen is a fine fabric popular in hot climates because it cools the body. For the linen to be viable, the flax had to be soaked for the pre-requisite amount of time, and then dried thoroughly so the fibers would separate. If one step was skipped the linen would either be of poor quality or not hold up when stitched. Lying under the fibers was a great place to hide because, had the guards gone to

Rahab's rooftop, all they would have seen was flax spread out. The layers of the stalks made it difficult to walk around.

Being industrious is a valuable quality, but what Rahab did for the spies took courage. She obviously lied to the guards by telling them the men had been there but had already left. Let's take a closer look at the lie, though. Harboring a known enemy of the state and protecting them would be considered an act of treason in any country, including our own. Treason is never taken lightly and almost always carries a heavy penalty—usually execution. Rahab risked her own life to protect the spies because she knew God was greater than any people or any king. She had heard the stories of what the Lord had done to bring the Israelites out of Egypt. She knew how powerful God is. She put her confidence in the Lord above that of the rulers of her own city. Rahab believed in the God of Abraham even though she only heard about him by second and third-hand accounts of his omnipotent actions in the desert. (Joshua 2:4)

We can't forget that Rahab was loyal to her family. We don't know what her relationship with them would have been, but her profession as a known prostitute could very well have served as a point of contention with her parents and siblings. When it was time to extract a promise of protection from the spies, she included her family. She didn't think only of herself. Her family was clearly important to her because she was purposeful in making sure they would also be saved from certain death at the hands of the invading Israelites. (Joshua 2:3–4)

All of the previous characteristics point out the fact that Rahab was obviously intelligent. When the two spies showed up at her door, she quickly came up with a plan to hide them. She was clever in sending the king's guard on a wild goose chase around the mountainous areas surrounding Jericho. Then Rahab gave specific instructions to the two men. They were to go into the mountains for three days. Only then could the spies return to the camp on the other side of the Jordan. She must have known the route the guardsmen would have taken to hunt down the Israelite spies. (Joshua 2:15–16)

RAHAB'S COURAGE

At this point, it would appear Rahab had no faults. The opposite is true. (Romans 3:23) She struggled with sin just like the rest of us. She was a prostitute living a lifestyle that, even today, is considered one of degradation and shame. Rahab would be the type of person we all might think of as undeserving of salvation. But her great sin is no greater than the "little" sins we commit daily. (Joshua 2:1)

As a result of Rahab's quick thinking and act of courage, she is one of two women listed with the heroes of the faith. Hebrews Chapter 11 begins with a definition of faith—"the substance of things hoped for, the evidence of things not seen." (v. 1) By faith Rahab believed all the Lord had done for the nation of Israel. God had heard the Hebrews' cries of despair and suffering. He sent Moses to Egypt as ambassador for his own people. The Lord brought ten plagues on Egypt, each one worse than the previous. When the angel of death went through killing the firstborn of every family, except for those whose doorposts and lintels were covered with lamb's blood, the Hebrews were finally allowed to leave Egypt. The stories of God's guidance during the desert wanderings led Rahab to understand the power of the Lord over every other god or idol. She knew the Israelites had finally arrived and would attack and conquer the city of Jericho. She understood God's power both to destroy and to save.

Rahab's life demonstrates the power of Light in a world darkened by sin. Her story affirms the Lord's power to save even the most depraved of people. Hopefully, none of us is engaged in a life like Rahab's. Let us remember, though, we are all sinners just like her. Let us remember that God's love and salvation are offered equally to everyone without distinction.

DISCUSSION QUESTIONS -

1. Rahab faced danger in extreme circumstances. Think - Would you do the same?

2. How can we emulate Rahab even though we are not in her situation?

PART 3

Women of Courage in Adversity

Deborah - Wise Warrior

*A wife of noble character who can find? She is worth far
more than rubies.*

PROVERBS 31:10

RECENT DEBATES OVER WOMEN'S roles in the church have prompted books about the topic, heated discussions, and often, hurt feelings. There exists the idea that a woman's only biblical function
in the church is taking a turn in the nursery or organizing the
monthly potluck dinner on a Sunday after the service. It's a well-
known leftover from a previous generation's philosophy of Christian service. Don't get me wrong, these are important ministries
and the women who serve in them are unsung heroes. But is that
all we're capable of? Are we fit only for that particular function?
Today's woman would say, "Of course not!"

Today, there are churches that take a more egalitarian approach. Women are welcome and encouraged to exercise any leadership role, including that of pastor or deacon. Several churches
in town have women pastors who have been ordained and bear
the title of Reverend. They have studied in a seminary of their de-
nomination and believe God has called them to the role of under-
shepherd of a church.

A third group encourages women to serve beyond the
nursery, potluck dinners and baby showers. This "in the middle"
group gives women the liberty to choose and explore where they

may fit in the ministries of the church as they consider their gifts and strengths. These may include leading worship, managing the Christian Education Department, handling monies, etc. However, the line is clearly drawn at the offices of pastor and deacon as noted in 1 Timothy 3.

The woman highlighted in this chapter was chosen by God to lead Israel during the time of the Judges. Whether we lean toward one faction or another, we cannot negate the fact that Deborah was a judge in Israel, chosen by God. As usual, it was during a troubling and turbulent time in Israel's history.

The Children of Israel had conquered the land God promised to Abraham, Isaac, and Jacob, largely under the leadership of Joshua. When he died, the Israelites were foundering, confused, and had forgotten the Law. They were doing what "was right in their own eyes." (Judges 17:6) The Lord appointed judges to lead the newly established nation and bring the people back into fellowship with God. So began the cycle. The people "did evil in the sight of the LORD." (Judges 3:7, etc.) God would choose a judge who would rule and the land would have rest. When the judge died, the people began the cycle again—"doing evil in the sight of the LORD."

The Israelites' apathy toward all things spiritual is prevalent throughout the book. The big difference between Moses and the judges is that Moses was a spiritual leader as well as a political one. The judges were political leaders who manifested spiritual maturity in their lives. Well, most of them.

DEBORAH'S STORY

Deborah's story is found in Judges chapters 4–5. If we look at a timeline of the judges, we'll see that some of the judges may have served at the same time. This is something we don't readily perceive when reading the texts. The unknown author of the book of Judges wrote about one judge at a time giving the idea they served sequentially. Some were called to judge over a few tribes rather than the whole nation. Transportation being what it was at the time made it difficult for a judge to carry out the "hands-on" directives from the Lord. People either traveled on foot or a slow moving four-legged animal. So, it seemed necessary to have judges over the other areas and tribes as well. Twelve are highlighted in the book of Judges.

Deborah was the only female judge God chose to lead the people. She most likely judged the people of Efraim, Naphtali and Zebulon and probably also judged at the same time as Gideon, Tola and Jair. There are some discrepancies between timelines so most of this is conjecture on my part. We'll call it an educated guess. What we do know is Deborah had to follow up on a task given to another person—Barak.

The curtain opens with Deborah under a palm tree called, interestingly enough, Deborah's palm tree. This palm tree served as her "office." It's where Deborah received people with cases to present, debate and for her to judge. She is introduced as a prophetess and the wife of Lapidoth. It is the only time Lapidoth is mentioned and nothing is known about him. His name, however, might give us a clue because it means *flame* or *torch*—a name given to men considered to be strong and brave.

The text gives no indication of Lapidoth's attitude toward Deborah's position of leadership as a judge. There is also no reason to believe there may have been conflict between Lapidoth and Deborah. Some may think this to be an unimportant piece of information. It's not important enough to have been included in the account, but it's not unreasonable to believe Deborah's marriage was stable enough to allow her to be an effective judge over the tribes of Israel.

We can conclude as well that Deborah was accepted as a judge because she was a prophetess. Being a prophet of God gave a person credibility and respect. She was constantly receiving messages from God which she related to the people. Deborah summoned Barak in Judges 4:6. The conversation she had with Barak was an example of her calling to be a prophetess. Deborah asked Barak why he hadn't obeyed the Lord's command to gather the army of 10,000 men at Mount Tabor. The Lord was going to draw

Sisera, the general of Jabin's army, out along with his battle-ready troops. Israel would defeat them. Barak responded with a request. He asked Deborah to accompany him and the troops when they went to attack Sisera.

Sisera was an intimidating opponent. His army possessed 900 iron chariots which required 900 horses. No other army had chariots made of iron making them more durable. The chariots also allowed the drivers to be elevated above foot soldiers giving them the advantage during battle—especially when the men on the ground were fighting with spears and shields. Neither were very effective against an iron chariot.

The chariots' speed also worked in Sisera's favor because a man on foot would never be able to outrun it. Any soldier attempting to flee would be run over with ease and another attempting to catch the chariot would never be able to overtake it. In other words, the Israelite army was grossly disadvantaged when it came to fighting Sisera's army and it's easy to understand Barak's reluctance to battle against it. However, it prompts us to conclude that Barak trusted Deborah more than he trusted God, the Creator of the universe. So, Deborah prophesied Israel's victory by a woman's hand and not Barak's. If we were to stop reading at this point, the conclusion might be that Deborah would be the one to defeat Sisera. However, as we continue with the narrative, we discover a yet unnamed woman would accomplish it instead.

DEBORAH'S CALLING

Why didn't Deborah lead the army into battle against Sisera? Deborah agreed to accompany Barak to the front of the battle because he was the general, not her. She may have stayed at a distance from the fighting, but this didn't mean she was safe. Deborah was a judge, a leader of people, not the general commanding an army. That position had been given to Barak and she respected it.

Deborah accepted the will of God that Barak would command the army and do all the fighting. It was neither her place nor her calling to be a warrior. She was content to serve the Lord within the parameters he had established for her. When we read the accounts of the other judges, they had been called to be in the fight against the enemy. Not Deborah. She was an exception. Deborah may have been capable of wielding a sword and protecting herself with a shield, but it was not what God had called her to do.

When Barak led the army into battle, God struck Sisera's warriors and chariot drivers with confusion. The enemy panicked and began to scatter in all directions making it easy for the Israelites to subdue them, chariots and all. Sisera, coward that he was, jumped out of his chariot and fled as fast and as far as he could go. When he saw tents in the distance, Sisera headed straight for them to seek refuge.

Jael, the wife of Heber, was there to receive Sisera and invited him into her tent. He was exhausted from the run and asked for water to drink. Then he ordered Jael to keep watch at the tent opening and warn him if the Israelites were coming. Jael's response was, "Here, have some milk instead." which Sisera gratefully accepted. As a Bedouin woman, Jael would most likely have given Sisera camel's milk which has a much higher fat content than cow's milk. The rich, thick drink would have made Sisera feel satisfied and drowsy. It wasn't long before he was sleeping soundly.

The Bedouin are a nomadic people moving from place to place to find pasture for their flocks of sheep. The women were responsible for pitching the tents when they arrived at a new location. Their tents were not the easy, toss-them-in-the-air and it would land gracefully, ready to use. The Bedouin put up their tents the old-fashioned way—by laying it out flat and driving stakes into the hard desert earth to secure it. This was no easy feat and the women who wielded the mallets were strong. While Sisera was sound asleep, Jael picked up an extra stake, placed it on his temple and drove that stake right through his skull and into the ground. Jael hit the stake with such force it only took a couple of strikes to push it through Sisera's skull. What a graphic picture! By this time, Barak was in the area looking for Sisera. Jael called to him and showed him the corpse in her tent.

That day Sisera's army was defeated and humiliated. God caused the panic that made the soldiers scatter and Jael eliminated the leader in a brutal attack. Barak walked away with no recognition for the victory whatsoever.

DEBORAH'S QUALIFICATIONS

Deborah's confidence in God and his plan cannot be denied. She knew what she could and couldn't do. A leader in a time of chaos needs these qualities. Effective leaders surround themselves with people who have different strengths than their own.

Barak's respect and deference toward Deborah were commendable. However, he had been given a clear task by God which he refused to perform without Deborah. As a result, a simple nomadic woman defeated an entire army with a tent stake. This left Deborah in an *"I told you so"* position. Instead, she and Barak sang a song of praise to the Lord for the victory over Sisera and his army at the hand of Jael.

Deborah was not the type of woman to boast and remind Barak of all the mistakes he had made. She was the type of woman to stand next to Barak and sing about the victory. She was humble and sang about all God had done that day. And she very likely returned to sit under her palm tree and listen to complaints and accusations, make judgements, and lead a people.

Women in leadership often find themselves in situations where humble leadership is necessary. Sometimes making decisions feels like walking a tightrope and one wrong step can cause a disastrous fall. Cool confidence in God's call and trust in his plan helps us to carefully put one foot in front of the other as we continue the treacherous crossing.

Women are intelligent and capable of taking leadership roles in the home, the church, and society. Let's be careful, though, to respect the parameters set down by God. It's important to know where the line is so we don't cross it. God sets boundaries to protect us, not imprison us. We must seek to stay within them.

DISCUSSION QUESTIONS

1. What situations in leadership do women find themselves today? Is this a good or bad thing and why?

2. What about you? Are you content in the situation God has placed you? Even though you may not have asked for it?

Ruth and Naomi - Picture of Redemption

But Ruth replied, "Don't urge me to leave you or to turn back from you. Where you go I will go, and where you stay I will stay. Your people will be my people and your God my God."

RUTH 1:16

SHORTLY AFTER MY HUSBAND, Doug, passed away, I sensed the Holy Spirit pushing me to return to ministry in Brazil. Frankly, the thought of updating my resume and searching for a job in today's working world terrified me. Ministry was familiar and so was Brazil. I knew how I could best contribute to the work and ministry with the churches. So far, it has been a good decision. There have been some hiccups, the Covid 19 Pandemic for example, but the Lord continues to steer me into the familiar. There's comfort in that and it was probably what Naomi was thinking, too.

To begin, imagine living in your hometown—the place where you were born and grew up. You've been married long enough to have two sons. Suddenly a famine strikes the land, the likes of which nobody has seen since the days when Joseph was in Egypt. This is how the book of Ruth begins.

During the time the judges ruled in Israel, a Bethlehemite, Elimelech, heard there was food in Moab. He summoned his wife, Naomi, and their two sons, Mahlon and Chilion, and set out from

Bethlehem to settle in that land. It's not certain how long they had been in Moab when Elimelech died leaving Naomi a widow.

Mahlon and Chilion married Moabite women. When they had been living in Moab for about ten years, Mahlon and Chilion died. Now, Naomi was not only a widow, but she was also childless. Her grief was profound and overwhelming leaving her utterly lost. With no one to support her, Naomi had no reliable source of income. To say Naomi was in a fix is an understatement. She was facing living on the street in abject poverty. So, Naomi decided to go back to Bethlehem. At least there were some people who knew her and might take pity on her in her hometown.

Grief can feel like an uphill mountain climb with quicksand along the path. When we experience the loss of a loved one, we carry the pain with us our entire lives. It never goes away and we don't "get over it." We learn to move forward carrying the dull ache in our hearts realizing life will never be the way it was before and we adapt to being a different person.

Sometimes it is so difficult to crawl out of those first stages of numbness, sadness, or denial. Some people seem to bounce back without much difficulty. They go back to work or dive into new activities occupying every minute of the day. Outward demeanor can be a facade which leads the observer to believe the one experiencing grief is doing well. They may be, but you can also be sure they are hurting on the inside. There is no right or wrong way to handle grief. It is a journey as individual and specific as the person experiencing it. They shouldn't be questioned or judged.

NAOMI'S DECISION

Naomi's grief was debilitating. She had lost her entire family and it is no wonder she decided to go back to Bethlehem. She was returning to take comfort in the familiar. The famine had left the land and the grain harvest would be well underway by the time she arrived. This made her decision to go home easier. She didn't count on her two daughters-in-law going with her, though.

As Naomi was preparing to leave for Bethlehem, her daughters-in-law, Orpah and Ruth, were also packing to go with her. Naomi protested their decision to accompany her stating they were young enough to remarry and bear children. They set out with Naomi anyway.

Along the way, Naomi again tried to convince the young women to return to Moab. At one point she even bitterly exclaimed her confusion as to why they would go with her. She had no more male offspring to offer the women. She was past the age to have more children. She had no idea what she would face when she arrived in Bethlehem. Maybe she didn't want the burden of having to care for Orpah and Ruth in a country foreign to them.

The law of Moses states in Deuteronomy 25:5, "If brothers are living together and one of them dies without a son, his widow must not marry outside the family. Her husband's brother shall take her and marry her and fulfill the duty of a brother-in-law to her." This is the concept of the Kinsman Redeemer and the major theme throughout the book of Ruth.

So, according to Mosaic Law, another son of the family was to marry his brother's widow and produce offspring. Children born to the widow were considered to be those of the brother who had died. The purpose was to perpetuate the line of every son born into a family. Naomi had no other sons to offer and no hope of having more children.

Finally, Orpah was convinced and went home to her family. Nothing more is said of her. Ruth, however, had a completely different attitude. She made a declaration of faith that seemingly came out of nowhere. However, Naomi's family must have demonstrated their own faith in the God of Abraham during their time in Moab and Ruth must have been watching. With conviction she said, "Your people shall be my people and your God my God." (Ruth 1:16) What could Naomi say to that? She turned and Ruth went with her all the way to Bethlehem.

At first glance, the first chapter of Ruth could be equal to any great tragedy written by Shakespeare. At the close of the chapter, Naomi and Ruth arrive in Bethlehem to the wonder of the residents who barely recognized Naomi. She confirmed her identity by asking the people not to call her Naomi but Mara which means "bitter." Naomi had returned home a defeated and embittered woman.

However, the last statement of the chapter is incongruous with everything else and sets off a spark of hope. Naomi and Ruth had arrived "at the beginning of the barley harvest." (Ruth 1:22) It's the cliffhanger that entices us to read on.

This book carries Ruth's name, but I've been of the opinion for quite some time that the protagonist and the one (spoiler alert) redeemed is Naomi. We'll get back to that a little later in the chapter. For now, we understand Ruth had a vital role in God's plan for the Kinsman Redeemer, but Naomi was the one who took the initiative in mentoring Ruth. The angry, bitter Naomi embraced her responsibility to counsel Ruth on how to go about bringing Boaz, the Kinsman Redeemer, around and accepting his role. This gives us an interesting insight into Naomi's influence and character.

NAOMI'S CHARACTER

The famine was ending and God was blessing the nation of Israel with food again. and we can determine by her quick resolution to return to Israel that Naomi was decisive. She had nothing left in Moab—at least nothing she wasn't willing to leave behind. She made her choice and went with it. Her husband and sons were gone. She had two daughters-in-law and no means to support them. She probably missed her friends back home. It was the logical decision to return.

Naomi's love for her daughters-in-law is evident when she asks for the Lord's blessing on them in Ruth 1:8. "Go, return each of you to her mother's house. May the LORD deal kindly with you, as you have dealt with the dead and with me." She thought returning them to their families was what was best for them. Naomi went on to say she hoped they would marry again. Marriage brought stability for a woman. In a culture where women gained value by their ability to have children, this was a sincere desire for Naomi to see Orpah and Ruth in a relationship that would guarantee a husband to love and take care of them, put a roof over their heads, and food on the table.

The glimmer of hope seen in the last sentence of chapter 1 becomes a bright light in chapter 2. It's also hope founded in wisdom. We could say Ruth lucked out when she landed in Boaz's field to gather grain. Or we could admit that God's powerful and purposeful sovereignty led Ruth there. Naomi's wisdom and understanding of Mosaic Law were the catalysts in prompting Boaz into action. (Ruth 2:20–23) Ruth benefitted by trusting Naomi and being with what was familiar.

NAOMI'S HOPE

The book bears Ruth's name, but she's been in a supporting role to this point. Ruth pretty much keeps that role even though she becomes more prominent in the narrative. Ruth's decision to accompany her mother-in-law by making a declaration of faith would change her life in ways she could not have imagined.

While Naomi was sending Orpah off with a hug and a kiss, we can imagine Ruth was girding herself for battle when Naomi said, "Look, Orpah's going back. Just go back with her." Envision Ruth facing off with Naomi in a stance reminiscent of a sumo wrestler preparing for a match. Ruth boldly declared, "I'm going where you go. I'm staying where you stay. I'm identifying myself with your people and I will worship your God as my God!" Obstinate. Sincere. Convicted. And loving! Words that silenced all of Naomi's protests.

RUTH'S CHARACTER

Ruth must have had to summon all the courage she could muster to prompt the words that expressed a true conversion to faith in the Lord. With those words, Naomi realized Ruth's determination to continue the journey with her. It turned out that Ruth's tenacity would bring great benefit to Naomi—both immediate and in the long term. Ruth's character was instrumental in the introduction of the Kinsman Redeemer, a provision for widows and a dead husband's land laid down in Mosaic Law. (Leviticus 25:25-28; Deuteronomy 25:5-6)

The law states that a male relative would take responsibility as the redeemer for the widow by marrying her and producing heirs. This man would also become owner of any land the husband possessed at the time of his death.

Christ as our brother is the Kinsman Redeemer in the New Testament (Hebrews 2:11). He is the one who bought us at a high price—his life—to make the church his bride. The best representation of the Kinsman Redeemer is in the book of Ruth. Her character and reputation contributed to Naomi's matchmaking.

After the two women settled in Bethlehem, Ruth went looking for work and food. A customary practice during the harvest was to allow the poor to walk behind the reapers and gather stalks that had been dropped and left behind. Ruth discovered this and quickly stepped in behind a reaper. She found herself in Boaz's field picking up as many stray stalks as she could. Unbeknownst to her, Boaz was well-known and respected among the people of Bethlehem.

When Boaz arrived at his field to check in with the workers, he noticed Ruth and asked who she was. Upon learning she was Naomi's daughter-in-law, he instructed the reapers to drop stalks on purpose to give her the opportunity to gather plenty to take home. It appears the two widows were also well-known. The people in town knew of the Moabite woman, Ruth, living with and providing for Naomi. At the end of the day, Ruth had enough grain to keep both women fed for a while.

Before Ruth left for home, Boaz told her to return only to his field to glean as it could be dangerous to do otherwise. Single women risked bodily harm when working in a field by themselves. When she arrived at their dwelling, Naomi discovered from whose field Ruth had gleaned. Naomi then gave specific instructions as to how to gain Boaz's attention and ask him to fulfill the role of the Kinsman Redeemer. Ruth obeyed by replying, "'All that you say I will do.'" (Ruth 3:5) She understood Naomi had a plan with a purpose that would benefit them both. Her trust in Naomi's counsel was unwavering. It's obvious from this incidence that Ruth followed the directions of the woman who knew more about life in Israel.

Ruth took Naomi's directives seriously. She bathed, put on her best garment, and went to the threshing floor where the men would spend the night to protect the grain from thieves. Ruth snuck in after they had gone to sleep, uncovered Boaz's feet and lay down to wait. Uncovering his feet was more practical than it was ceremonial. Logically, Boaz would awaken when his feet got cold.

Sometime later, Boaz awoke with a start and found Ruth lying there. When questioned, Ruth asked Boaz to "'spread your wings over your servant, for you are a redeemer.'" (Ruth 3:9b) These seem like confusing words, but Ruth was, in a manner, proposing marriage to Boaz. His response was to bless her because she did what was culturally correct instead of seeking out a younger man. There are indications Boaz was over forty years old, while Ruth would have been much younger.

That bold action on Ruth's part prompted Boaz to accept his role as Kinsman Redeemer and to take the place of Naomi's son, Mahlon. Ruth and Boaz were married soon after her visit to the threshing floor. At least nine months later, their first child was born, a son named Obed who is identified as King David's grandfather in the subsequent genealogy.

Naomi became Obed's nurse and the women of Bethlehem announced, "'Blessed be the LORD, who has not left you this day without a redeemer, and may his name be renowned in Israel!'" (Ruth 4:14) and "'A son has been born to Naomi.'" (Ruth 4:17) Naomi was redeemed through Ruth's obedience and Boaz's willingness.

The narrative closes with the genealogy of David, second king of Israel, the man after God's own heart. David was the man with whom God made an unconditional covenant by promising a descendent on the throne of Israel forever. In other words, there was nothing anyone could do to break the covenant. It was solely on God to fulfill.

When reading the genealogy of Jesus Christ in Matthew 1, David is listed as a direct descendent of Boaz and Jesus as a direct descendent of David. This was to confirm Jesus is the Messiah that was promised in the covenant. The ultimate promise of the covenant has not been fulfilled. In the future, Jesus will be crowned King and will reign forever. (Rev 19:16) And it all started with one young, foreign woman who declared her complete, unwavering trust in the God she could not see.

Sometimes we struggle with pride when it comes to considering the advice of elders and receiving their counsel or suggestions with grace. Naomi realized her responsibility in instructing Ruth. And Ruth, in turn, realized her responsibility in respecting and acting on the older woman's advice. Ruth embraced and followed Naomi's orders to the letter because she trusted God, and Naomi as well. Ruth had the wisdom to discern and value the perspectives of others in situations and customs foreign to her. She allowed an older, more experienced woman (Naomi), to guide her on a path to redemption. Naomi lived Titus 2:3 as she mentored Ruth. As a result, a nation was blessed.

DISCUSSION QUESTIONS

1. Why do you think God would choose two non-Israelite women (Rahab and Ruth) to continue the Davidic and Messianic line?

2. Explain how this story is more about Naomi's redemption than Ruth's?

Hannah - Hope in Adversity

*Eli answered, "Go in peace, and may the God of Israel grant
you what you have asked of him."*

1 SAMUEL 1:17

EXPLORING THE LIFE OF Hannah brings with it two depressing
circumstances that afflicted her. First, she was not able to have
children which greatly affected her role in the family and how
society perceived her. Second, Hannah was one of two wives. The
husband, Elkanah, needed heirs. Hannah could not have children.
Elkanah married Peninnah who bore him several children. This
caused Hannah anguish even though she was the wife Elkanah
loved.

Infertility is one of those unfortunate circumstances that can
take a toll on a couple who desire to have children. Many seek the
care of a physician who can prescribe medications that stimulate
hormones into action. Other couples will develop their own meth-
od of counting days, taking temperatures and disrupting their
schedules in the hopes they will successfully have a child. At some
point the two will empty their bank accounts to attempt IVF (In
Vitro Fertilization) or begin the adoption process. The stress can
bring a marriage to ruin. It can also bring the two closer together.
Either way, infertility has a way of turning even the most patient
and tranquil of people into short-tempered, angry individuals. It's

even worse when a man finds another woman who is not only fertile but is able to bear him several children.

When reading accounts of polygamy in the Bible most people have a tendency to cringe and shake their heads because it seems to be such a foreign concept. It's difficult to imagine having to share a spouse with another person. Even thinking about the subject brings on feelings of indignation and possessiveness. The practice of polygamy was declared unlawful in the US in 1882. Today it is illegal in every state of the Union. Current mainstream American culture has generally rejected the idea and most marriages are monogamous; most being the operative word.

The fact is, there are several religious groups in the USA that encourage polygamous "marriages." It's difficult to know if there is an official registry in a government facility. The relationships could, at best, be considered common law marriages between several people, although every state has its own legislation concerning common law. These contracts usually involve one man having several wives and many children. Polygamy is often oppressive for the women who are forced to live in one dwelling bringing up their children together with those of other "wives." Some of these women are able to escape the life with the help of outside organizations. Others think it is better to stay with the husband because life outside the bounds of the compound terrifies them.

In the Old Testament polygamy was a common practice. Jacob had four wives who gave him twelve male offspring. King David collected wives after making them widows. King Solomon had 700 wives and 300 concubines. The practice seems to have died out by the time Jesus came into the world which started the New Testament era.

HANNAH'S ANGUISH

As mentioned, Jacob had two wives and two concubines who could also be considered wives. He had to work for his father-in-law, Laban, for seven years to marry Rachel the younger sister. On the wedding night, Laban sent Rachel's sister, Leah, into Jacob's tent instead. The ruse worked because Leah's face was covered with a veil which was not removed until the following morning. The deceit was so disconcerting that Jacob confronted Laban who explained to Jacob it was improper for the younger daughter to marry before the older. Jacob loved Rachel and still wanted her as his wife so he worked another seven years to marry her. The two women were jealous of each other and competed to have as many children as possible. They each gave Jacob their personal slaves, Bilhah and Zilpah. Jacob ended up with four women to support along with their children.

Rachel was barren and it was many years before she had children. Her oldest, Joseph, would become a great man in Egypt and save his family from extinction. Rachel died giving birth to her second son who was named Benjamin. But Joseph was Jacob's favorite child because he was the first child of the woman he truly loved.

The polygamous marriage described in 1 Samuel Chapter 1 is another example of a family dynamic full of conflict. Elkanah, a wealthy man from the hills of Ephraim, had two wives, Peninnah and Hannah. Just as in Jacob's case, Elkanah loved Hannah, the wife who was barren. This caused bitter jealousy between the two women.

Elkanah went yearly from Ramah in the region of Ephraim to Shiloh (the location of the Tabernacle) to offer sacrifices with his entire family. He gave Peninnah and each of her children a portion to sacrifice, but to Hannah, he gave a double portion because he loved her.

The conflict between the two women was fierce. Peninnah had all the children and Hannah had none. In the ancient world's eyes Hannah was worthless which made it acceptable for Elkanah to have another wife so he could have heirs. Peninnah was angry and bitter to the point of verbally attacking Hannah reminding her constantly of her insignificance. Hannah was distressed to the point of tears which led her husband to ask her, "'Hannah, why do you weep? And why do you not eat? And why is your heart sad? Am I not more to you than ten sons?'" (1 Samuel 1:8) Elkanah felt that Hannah should be content with his love for her. It didn't matter to him that she had no children so it shouldn't have mattered to her. It sounds a bit like a rebuke.

Naturally, Hannah was crying all the time and wouldn't eat. She was profoundly sad because of her circumstances. Her anguish consumed her thoughts and was visible on her face. Hannah's home life was truly miserable having to put up with Peninnah's constant verbal abuse. However, Hannah's story in 1 Samuel gives us hope which seems counterintuitive with what is in the account to this point. Let's take a look at the rest of the narrative.

It's pretty obvious Hannah lived in a culture of conflicting standards. To the world, Hannah's infertility reduced her to an undesirable woman with little to offer society. Of course, infertility was usually only discovered after the marriage had taken place. If the couple did not have any children after an appropriate amount of time, the man would find another woman who could give him children. It was accepted and legal.

God's standard for Hannah was different, though. 1 Samuel 1:5-6 makes it clear; the LORD had closed her womb. It's such an important factor that it's mentioned twice. God had a purpose and a plan. He used the occasion to work in Hannah's life, but she needed an attitude change before he would begin the work. God's standard for Hannah was that she seek him first and trust him to accomplish his will. He wanted Hannah to focus on her spiritual condition rather than her physical.

Hannah's unsettling home life was a burden she bore daily. She was constantly ridiculed by Peninnah who declared she had no value. Peninnah sought to provoke Hannah at every turn reminding her of her inability to have children. It's reasonable to believe Peninnah's children got in on the abuse. The servants may have had little respect for a woman who was barren. And this went on for years. Who wouldn't be in the pit of depression while enduring such relentless mockery?

Hannah's story took place during the time of the judges, just like Deborah's, Ruth's and Naomi's. The nation of Israel was in a constant cycle of turning its back on the Lord, then crying out for deliverance when the enemy oppressed. God would raise up a judge and give the people peace for a time. In other words, Elkanah and his family were living among a degenerate people because "In those days there was no king in Israel. Everyone did what was right in his own eyes." (Judges 21:25)

Hannah's condition was not unique to her. There are several other accounts in the Scriptures telling the stories of women who couldn't bear children. Remember Sarah and Rebekah? There were most likely other women in other regions experiencing the same anguish, the same circumstances, the same depression which can manifest itself in different ways.

Many who are depressed, regardless of the circumstances, comfort themselves with food while others can't stand the thought of eating. Some sleep up to twenty hours a day while others suffer from insomnia. Some haven't the energy to get off the couch and others won't stop to sit because they don't want to think. Symptoms are as varied as weather patterns. Hannah suffered from depression and it crushed her spirit.

HANNAH'S RESPONSE

During supper one evening in Shiloh, Hannah found herself at the end of her rope. She couldn't stop crying and wouldn't eat. By now Elkanah was getting concerned and asked her what was upsetting her so. Then he asked the question that would seem incredibly insensitive. "'Am I not more to you than ten sons?'" (1Sam 1:8) Why would Elkanah put the focus back on himself instead of dealing with Peninnah?

Hannah needed to put things in perspective and Elkanah's statement did just that. Instead of obsessing over her infertility, she should have been seeing to her responsibilities within the family and especially her husband. Maybe Hannah was inciting conflict with her husband by forever muttering about her circumstances. We don't know because it's not stated in the text, but after dinner Hannah finally made a wise decision. She went out to have a conversation with the Lord. She headed toward the Tabernacle where she knew she would find him.

Eli was seated at the doorway of the Tabernacle. Hannah fell to her knees nearby and began to pour her heart out to God. By this time Hannah was sobbing uncontrollably. With tears streaming down her face, she silently prayed forming the words with her lips. In this prayer she made a vow to the Lord. If God would give her a son, Hannah would give him back to the Lord to serve him for life. A bold declaration.

When we find ourselves in desperate circumstances it is easy to call on God to help us. We make bargains and promises that, in the end, are impossible to keep. There are not many women who would actually follow through on a promise such as the one Hannah made. She was navigating dangerous waters.

As Eli observed her unabashedly silent plea, he interpreted her demeanor as someone who had been drinking and he rebuked her. It would be inappropriate and audacious for Hannah to approach the throne of grace in that condition. However, Hannah respectfully replied she had been praying because of her "'anxiety and vexation.'" (1Sam 1:16)

Eli responded with a blessing. "'Go in peace, and the God of Israel grant your petition that you have made to him.'" (1 Sam 1:17) Hannah felt the burden lift. She rose to her feet, went and ate some food, and her facial expression changed to that of one who was happy, satisfied, and hopeful. She no longer obsessed.

We have to stop here and ask ourselves some questions. Had Hannah's life circumstances changed? No, they had not. How was she able to walk away from that prayer a different person? The Lord had changed her heart and she was able to focus on him rather than herself. How do we know this? Because Hannah "went her way and ate, and her face was no longer sad." (1 Sam 1:18b)

A few days later, Elkanah packed up his family and headed home. Peninnah was probably still relentless in antagonizing Hannah. The children and servants probably were too. Elkanah continued to favor Hannah over Peninnah. And Hannah probably still cried and poured her heart out to God.

In due time, though, Hannah became pregnant and had a son. She named him Samuel which means "'I have asked for him from the Lord.'" (1Sam 1:20). When it was time again to make the journey to Shiloh, Hannah told her husband she would not go to sacrifice again until Samuel was weaned. She would have her son with her for only three or four short years. After that, she would take Samuel to Shiloh to leave him in Eli's hands to be trained to serve the Lord as a priest in the Tabernacle. Hannah followed through on her vow.

Hannah must have had a tremendous amount of courage to turn Samuel over to the Lord thus fulfilling her vow. What woman wants to give up her child? Hannah learned an important lesson on that particular trip to Shiloh. She realized her focus was not on the Lord, where it should have been. This led her to fall before the Lord to make her request and vow. In her distress she held nothing back. She laid it all out before God and asked for a child and deliverance from infertility. She walked away with no guarantees, only a blessing from Eli. God heard and answered.

Hannah's faith and faithfulness in fulfilling her promise to the Lord in returning Samuel to the Lord's service could be one reason why he was one of the greatest leaders in Israel. A man who, in his youth, heard the voice of God and prophesied to Eli. He served as high priest in the Tabernacle, judged the nation of Israel, and crowned two of its kings. And he served God to the end of his days.

Would I have the courage and faith to do as Hannah did? I don't know, but I will say this. I did learn the hard way that my children belong to God. My son, Alex's senior year of high school in Brazil was a tough one for our family. Shortly after the school year began, he mentioned that there was something growing in his nose. I looked with a flashlight and sure enough, there it was. Doctors' visits and imaging revealed a mass in his sinus. This involved a trip to the coast to consult with a surgeon. After an hour or so into the surgery one of the staff came out to tell us it was a fungus. My son had a giant mushroom growing in his sinus cavity. That started us on a journey to manage allergies we didn't know he had.

Then a few months later, Alex and his older cousin, Dan, were abducted at gunpoint and taken on a 45-minute wild ride through the city only to be dumped in a field on their knees facing away from their attackers. They had been stripped of their shirts, wallets, cellphones and car keys. My husband and I found out about it after they had returned to the school complex. We all suffered from PTSD from the incident. It took us a long time to recover.

When Alex dislocated his elbow close to the end of the school year, I hardly reacted. My husband, Doug, had gone to the hospital with him and Dan picked me up to take me. Dan asked if I was alright. I said, "Are you kidding? This is nothing compared to what we've already experienced!"

Needless to say, when graduation rolled around, I fell apart. There were so many times during that year I wasn't sure Alex would make it to his graduation day, but I learned an important lesson. I finally understood that my children do not belong to me. They belong to God. I can try to protect them, but the Lord is the one that truly keeps them safe. I can teach them, but what they understand about life ultimately comes from God. Hannah had no other choice but to give Samuel completely over to the Lord. And neither did I.

DISCUSSION QUESTION

1. Why was Hannah able to go back to her family and life with her "face no longer sad"?

PART 4

Women Who Walked with Jesus

Mary - Mother of Jesus

The angel went to her and said, "Greetings, you who are highly favored! The Lord is with you."

LUKE 1:28

IT HAD BEEN FOUR hundred years since God last spoke to the people of Israel which are referred to as the Intertestamental Period because it happened between the close of the Old Testament and the beginning of the New Testament. There are reliable non-biblical sources that tell the history of Israel during those years. They divulge a time of great turmoil and suffering as a result of being occupied by many nations. As the New Testament era began, Israel was under the rule of Rome.

The first chapter of the Gospel of Luke relates the story of Elizabeth and Zechariah, the parents of John the Baptist. This chapter segues into the archangel Gabriel's visit with Mary, the betrothed of Joseph, a carpenter from Nazareth in the Galilee region. The chapter also tells the story of Mary's visit to Elizabeth in which the child in the older woman's womb jumped for joy at the younger woman's arrival. Mary's response was a hymn of praise, called the Magnificat, offered to the Lord. Moving on to Luke chapter two brings us to the account of the birth of Jesus Christ.

MARY'S STORY

All four gospels begin with the birth of Jesus in some way or other. Matthew's Gospel lists the twenty-eight generations from Adam to Christ. Mark's Gospel begins with the story of John the Baptist, Jesus' cousin, whose sole ministry was to prepare the way for Jesus' ministry. John the Baptist also baptized Jesus just before he went into the wilderness to be tempted by Satan. The Gospel of John starts with the beginning, before time, before creation. Jesus existed in eternity past making him a divine being and one with God.

A look at Luke 1:26-38 relates the conversation between the archangel, Gabriel, and Mary. It's a surprising conversation for a few reasons. First, God was breaking his four-hundred-year silence. There had been no new revelation during that time, nor any angelic visits. So, when an angel suddenly appeared to Mary, a teenage girl, she was at the very least surprised and at most scared out of her mind. Her reaction was probably closer to the latter since the first words out of Gabriel's mouth were, "'Do not be afraid . . .'" (Luke 1:30).

Gabriel went on to say Mary had found favor with God because she'd been chosen to be the mother of the Lord Jesus Christ. The problem with that revelation was that Mary was a virgin, and even though she was engaged to Joseph, they did not have a sexual relationship. Mary was most likely 14 or 15-years-old and, in the culture of that day, it wasn't unusual for a girl that young to marry and begin to have children. It would seem almost appalling in today's culture, but the fact she was engaged was a minor detail.

When the angel announced her impending pregnancy, Mary was confused. She knew how reproduction worked and that a man had to be involved. Mary knew it was impossible for her to be carrying a child. She hadn't counted on the Holy Spirit's part in this miracle because that's how she became pregnant.

It wasn't long before the rumors started and it became necessary for Joseph to confront Mary's family. He was a just man, though, and to keep Mary from being put to death by stoning, he resolved to break the contract quietly with just her family present.

Before Joseph could act on it, the angel Gabriel visited him and told him the child was of the Holy Spirit and that he should honor the marriage contract. Joseph and Mary became husband and wife.

At that time Israel was under Roman rule, and came to the notice of the emperor, Caesar Augustus, back in Rome. Caesar decided it was time to do a census and get an idea of the current population in Israel. There were probably a couple of reasons for this. First, he wouldn't want the population to become more numerous than the Romans. Otherwise, the nation could fight for their independence. Second, an accurate count would allow the government to raise taxes.

The census required that the head of each family must travel to his birthplace if necessary. In this case, Joseph had to make the journey from Nazareth to Bethlehem. The fact Mary was close to giving birth, made the trip extremely difficult. When they arrived in Bethlehem, not one inn had a place for them. Finally, one innkeeper took pity on them and offered them the stable where the guests sheltered their animals for the night.

The stalls were dirty and smelly. It's hard to believe anyone could bring a child into the world under those circumstances, but Mary did because she had no other choice. That baby was on his way. Jesus was born sometime during the night and, after cleaning him up a little, Mary swaddled him in some clean cloths and laid him in the animals' food trough. Under the circumstances, it was the best she could do.

Meanwhile, shepherds were in the surrounding fields keeping watch over their flocks of sheep. These were probably the sheep for the sacrifices during the Jewish festivals throughout the year. The sheep had to be without blemish so the shepherds kept careful eyes on the livestock because it was dark and predators were everywhere.

Suddenly, an angel appeared, lighting up the sky. Again, remember God had been silent for four hundred years and the angel was obliged to say, "'Fear not'" (Luke 2:10). He then informed the shepherds of Christ's birth in Bethlehem, where to find the stable, and what to expect. Gabriel's message ended with a choir of angels shouting praises to God. The shepherds went and found everything exactly as the angel had said.

MARY'S CHARACTER

Mary's story brings many questions to mind. Why did God choose her, a young teenager, to be the mother of our Lord? Why did she have to be a virgin and engaged to be married? Surely there were other young virgins who were descendants of David. The Lord had made a covenant with King David and promised a descendent on the throne of Israel for Eternity. Did God choose Joseph and Mary because they were people of integrity and lived lives pleasing to the Lord? Character had a lot to do with God's choice for Jesus' mother and adoptive father. Four characteristics that Mary displayed are wisdom beyond her years, scholarly endeavors, devotion to God with worship and praise, and genuine humility.

Mary's wisdom beyond her years shines as she deals with being visited by Gabriel to dealing with a pregnancy before marriage to the life and death of Jesus. She was with Jesus his entire life.

The mother of our Lord was also an Old Testament scholar. This passage in Luke 1:46–55 has eighteen discernible Old Testament quotes which leave little doubt Mary knew the Scriptures and practiced its teachings. Here's a list:

- Luke 1:46-47 - Ps 34:2–3; Hab 3:18
- Luke 1:48 - 1 Sam 1:11; Ps 138:6
- Luke 1:49 - Ps 71:19; 126:2–3; 111:9
- Luke 1:50 - Gen 17:7; Ps 103:17
- Luke 1:51a - Ps 98:1; 118:15; Is 40:10
- Luke 1:51b-52 - Ps 33:10; 1 Sam 2:7,8
- Luke 1:54 - Is 41:8; Ps 98:3
- Luke 1:55 - Gen 17:19; Ps 132:11

In contrast to God's worthiness to receive praise and honor, Mary recognized her own unworthiness. The angel, Gabriel, announced that she would be favored among women. She would be forever called blessed. Mary's response? "'He (God) has looked on the humble state of his servant'" (Luke 1:48). It was a big deal to be chosen to be the mother of the Redeemer, but Mary didn't let it go to her head.

Her humility came from a recognition of her dependence on God. The Holy Spirit put the child in her womb and Mary declared her dependence on the Lord by saying, "'He who is mighty has done great things for me'" (Luke 1:49). It was a wonderful miracle God was about to perform. Mary understood, without question, she was a recipient of a great blessing.

Public and private worship should be manifested in our lives so others may see our joy at being a child of God. Children should see their parents worshiping, praising God, his greatness and awesome power. This in turn should produce joy on the part of the worshipper. Parents who show disinterest and apathy toward the things of God will bring up disinterested and apathetic children. I love to look around in church and see families worshiping together. Parents and their children stand side by side singing and raising their hands in praise. Then they bow their heads as a family during prayer. This image brings back memories of my own family in Brazil as we sat together in church on Sundays. On other days, our children would observe Doug and me studying for upcoming speaking opportunities. We wanted them to see that our relationship with the Lord was genuine.

One of my husband's fondest memories of growing up in Brazil was seeing his mother sit in her favorite chair in a corner of her bedroom with a small table alongside. On the table were a lamp, a coaster, and her Bible. She would sit there daily to read and pray, all while sipping on a steaming cup of coffee. She rarely drank anything different during that time. It was always a cup of very hot coffee. Doug, a young child, observed this routine and called it "Mom's coffee cup Bible." That unassuming custom influenced her son to surrender his life to serving the Lord on the mission field.

Mary was chosen to be our Lord's mother because she was humble and willing to serve. She knew the Scriptures making it likely she knew the prophecy of Jesus' birth. She praised God even though she would be in a very precarious situation with the Jewish leaders. She accepted the challenge of a long journey south to Bethlehem only to give birth in a stable. She was a woman of character.

Mary was the perfect choice for the mother of our Lord. We should seek to adorn ourselves with Mary's characteristics. Be an example to your children. Let them see you studying your Bible and praying on a regular basis. Aspire to be the mother whose children will "rise up and call her blessed" (Proverbs 31:28a). Mary's examples of wisdom beyond her years, scholarly endeavors, devotion to God with worship and praise, and genuine humility made her God's best choice for the mother of our Lord.

DISCUSSION QUESTIONS

1. Fast forward to Luke 2:19, "But Mary treasured up all these things, pondering them in her heart." What is Mary's state of mind?

2. Are there indications that Mary didn't fully comprehend all that had happened and the significance of it?

Mary and Martha - Complete Opposites/Faithful Servants

"Martha, Martha," the Lord answered, "you are worried and upset about many things."

LUKE 10:41

I LOVE OVERHEARING CONVERSATIONS between young mothers comparing notes on potty training, cloth versus disposable diapers, which car seat is best, etc. One young mother in my church will very often send me texts of the latest phrase to come out of one of her girls' mouth. They can be doozies. My favorite to date was from the youngest who said, "My mom likes cows and unicorns."

Mothers will often talk about how one child differs from another. Some families have calm children, while others have very active ones. The families with special needs children have an extra set of challenges when it comes to the care of those precious souls. It's safe to say all parents would agree that every child has characteristics both similar and different from their siblings.

On the day my daughter was born I was surprised to see her face looked exactly like her brother's face on his first day. When I browse through photo albums today it's difficult for me to know which photo is of which child. The doctor and surgical team were the same. We were in the same operating room in the same hospital where our son was born. So it is hard to tell which birth is which. My son had a birthmark on his right cheek that could be seen in some pictures which helped me tell the difference between them.

There were the obvious differences such as, my oldest is a boy and my youngest is a girl and there's a three-and-a-half-year gap between them. My boy was also a pound and a half heavier than my daughter at birth. He was late. She was early. And we put obviously boy clothes on our son and obviously girl clothes on our daughter.

My kids were different physically, but they were also vastly different in other ways from the day they were born. My son had to be rocked to sleep. My daughter preferred to be put down and left alone. My son had some food allergies. My daughter didn't. My son grew to be tall. My daughter is not. My son is grounded. My daughter often has her head in the clouds dreaming of something wonderful. And they are both my children.

As they grew, their personalities took different directions as well. My son is calm under pressure and logically analyzes everything. He is introspective. My daughter is a drama queen who analyzes things by her emotions. She is the extrovert.

Today, their personalities have contributed to their work environments. My son writes software for assembly lines. My daughter is the operations manager at a company that handles HOAs (Home Owners Association) for housing complexes. They have their unique personality traits and use them in their jobs. They're both very good at what they do to earn a living. What makes me most grateful is they both actively serve in their churches.

Whether siblings are alike or different, there is always a recipe for chaos and conflict. One stole the other's colored pencils. The other one took the last french fry. One minute they're getting along like best friends, the next they're screaming and crying. It can go from peace to outright war in an instant. This is the "blessing" of family dynamics.

PORTRAIT OF TWO SISTERS

Mary and Martha were sisters who were completely different in personality and priority. These two women and their brother, Lazarus, were very good friends with Jesus and the Lord made a point to stop and visit the three siblings whenever he was in the area of Bethany. It's safe to assume Jesus stopped in often due to Bethany's proximity to Jerusalem. At least once a year our Lord passed through on his way to Jerusalem to celebrate Passover. One such visit resulted in conflict between the sisters and Jesus had to step in . . . well, let's say he was pulled in.

We learn a little about Mary and Martha as individuals and see that Martha was most likely the older of the two sisters. We come to this conclusion because she had command over the household. As the older sister she would have been considered wiser, more life-experienced, and the one in charge of managing the daily tasks and activities. Martha also considered it important to follow traditions set down by generations before. She took her role as female leader in the house very seriously. Therefore, housekeeping was a priority. Serving guests was a priority. She was the one to receive Jesus into her home by greeting him at the door. Martha would have offered the basin of water for Jesus to wash his hands and feet before entering the home. She would have ushered him in and given him the best seat at the table she was preparing.

In contrast, Mary was probably the younger sister who was less concerned with traditions and her role as a woman in the household, a role she would have shared with Martha. As Jesus came into her home to take his place at the table, she calmly sat down with the others (all men) to hear his words because he took every opportunity to teach the people. This action of Mary's may have set the men on edge as it was not common for women to sit at the table with the men. Under normal circumstances, Martha and Mary would have served the meal and retired to the kitchen to eat their dinner.

While Martha prepared the feast with her carefully chosen ingredients and bustled around the house, Mary sat at Jesus' feet while he conversed with the other men and taught them. Martha became increasingly irritated with her sister. This brings a memory to my own mind.

My husband and I were very often invited for a meal at the home of one of our church members, a common practice in Brazil where we served as missionaries. The people who attended our church were usually poor, which made the invitation special.

These faithful women would go to the market and spend more than they normally would have for their families on a cut of beef or a whole chicken. They would prepare the food, seasoning it with the best ingredients. As the beans and meat were cooking, they busied themselves with the complementary dishes they would serve.

The table was covered with a tablecloth stored in the back of the closet. It was rarely used, except when they had special guests. Our hostess rummaged through the plates searching for the ones without chips on the edges which would be a variety of colors and patterns. Lastly, the hostess pulled out her stainless-steel serving dishes. These are considered the "Fine China" of Brazil and everyone has a few. I still have some I brought back to the US with me. As the hostess would put the food on the table, one of the children took some cash and ran to the corner mercantile to purchase an ice cold two-liter Coca Cola. When the Coke arrived we knew this was to be a truly special meal.

What's my point? We all have a desire to impress our important house guests, like those women from the church. They loved to invite my husband, Doug, into their homes because they knew how much he appreciated it. When I was traveling and left him on his own, the women would invite him for several meals. Really, they gathered around him and clucked like hens taking care of their chicks.

Many times, these women, like Martha, were more concerned with putting on a great meal, and quite frankly, trying to outdo each other, than they were in taking time to visit with Doug. Their priorities were misplaced. They were concentrating on the temporal and not concerning themselves with the eternal.

DIFFERENT PRIORITIES

Martha was clearly irritated with Mary. Martha worked hard to put a meal together to serve her Lord and Savior while her sister sat idly by soaking in every word that came from Jesus' mouth. Martha probably wasn't even listening to Jesus' words because of her consternation.

Finally, Martha had had enough. Like a petulant child, she demanded that Jesus order Mary to help with meal preparations. She even rebuked him to some extent with, "'Lord, do you not care that my sister has left me to serve alone? Tell her to help me.'" (Luke 10:40) Did Martha really think Jesus hadn't noticed she was working alone?

Jesus surprised Martha by gently pointing out her distraction over temporal things. We can conclude from this that Jesus cared very little about food and keeping mealtimes. He was more concerned with his mission, especially when time was running out. Martha wasn't necessarily doing anything wrong. As a matter of fact, she was doing as she should have, preparing sustenance for a weary guest. It's noble to want to serve a good meal to a special guest. At that moment, though, Martha's priorities were confused. Jesus would have been more satisfied if Martha had stopped worrying about the food and paid more attention to his words.

In keeping with Mary's seeming disregard for tradition, she chose to continue at Jesus' feet, engrossed in every word he said. When she should have been helping her sister, she became oblivious to all that went on around her and focused on Jesus. Amid the clatter of pot lids and spoons stirring the bubbling stew over the fire, amid the swish, swish of the broom gathering dirt off the floor, Mary appeared absorbed with Jesus. She had tuned everything else out. Mary made a point to learn all she could from Jesus whenever she had the chance. Because Mary was so observant of Jesus' comings and goings as well as his teachings, she may have had a sense of what was to come. The other two incidents in which the sisters appear indicate Mary was probably so in tune with Jesus' words, she could have sensed the end was coming.

Later, when Mary broke into a gathering of men and proceeded to anoint Jesus' feet with costly perfume from an alabaster jar, she cared little about appearances. Mary was focused only on Jesus. She then wiped Jesus' feet with her hair. Judas looked on with disdain rebuking Jesus for not saving the precious oil to sell to fill their purse. However, Mary must have intuitively understood Jesus' time on earth was ending and she needed to take advantage of every moment. Therefore, she anointed his feet which had meaning beyond the understanding of anyone else in that room. "Jesus said, 'Leave her alone, so that she may keep it for the day of my burial.'" (John 12:7)

THE SAME FAITH

The tension and strife between the sisters were palpable, but Martha and Mary had something in common, their faith in Jesus Christ. In fact, their faith was so strong and sure that as soon as their brother, Lazarus, became ill, they sent someone to find Jesus and bring him back to heal their brother. When the messengers found Jesus on the other side of the Jordan near where his cousin, John, baptized the people, they notified him of Lazarus' condition. Appearing indifferent, Jesus didn't go to the sisters right away. He waited two more days. Lazarus was already dead by the time Jesus set out for Bethany.

The Lord finally showed up four days after Lazarus had been buried. The odor coming from the tomb would have been unbearable keeping mourners away. Martha and Mary were perplexed that Jesus had taken so long to come after alerting him to Lazarus' condition.

When Martha heard Jesus was arriving, she immediately took off to meet him on the road. Her frustration would have been obvious when she said, "'Lord, if you had been here, my brother would not have died.'" (John 11:21) Now, Martha understood Jesus' power over death. She had been listening when he talked about death and the resurrection. She believed Jesus was "'the Christ, the Son of God.'" (John 11:27) Jesus reassured Martha with "'Your brother will rise again.'" (John 11:23)

While Martha was having a conversation with Jesus on the road, Mary was at home with the other mourners. It wasn't until Martha returned with the news Jesus had summoned her that Mary went to meet him. As Mary reached Jesus, she fell at his feet. It's interesting to note here that in every encounter Mary had with Jesus, she was on her knees before him. This is significant behavior because it demonstrates Mary's humility and worship of her Savior.

Mary repeated Martha's statement. "'Lord, if you had been here, my brother would not have died.'" It's at this point Jesus observed the grieving people around him. He asked to be taken to the tomb and, upon arrival, Jesus let loose his own grief and he wept. (John 11:35) He was overcome with emotion and overwhelmed with grief because of what death had brought to this world overrun with sin.

Both women believed in the future resurrection of the dead as Jesus had taught them and when he mentioned that Lazarus would live again, Martha thought Jesus spoke of that event. They also believed Jesus had the power to keep Lazarus from dying because they knew the many stories of Jesus healing the infirmed. They confessed Jesus was the Christ, the Messiah. However, they both must have been stunned to silence when they heard Jesus' command, "'Lazarus, come out!'" (John 11:43). Within seconds Lazarus came shuffling out of the tomb still wrapped in burial linens. The Lord had just performed his most powerful miracle to date. A man who had been dead four days came back to life at Jesus' words. A body in active decomposition was revived and breathed again.

Two women with different perspectives received an exorbitant blessing from God. Their brother was alive again! Sisters with different outlooks on life agreed on their faith in Jesus Christ. They had learned an important lesson on priorities.

As we contemplate our own lives, we have to ask, "Are my priorities right?" "Is my focus on Christ first and other things second?" "Do I need to get on my knees?" Putting priorities in order is almost a cliché these days. It is important, though. Christ must be the main focus of our lives. Everything we do and say, our attitudes and how we live, must all reflect Christ's active role as sole focus in our day-to-day living.

As different as we all may be, we all have something in common. We offer our time, our gifts, our service to God whether we are older and more experienced or younger with much to learn. We're not all the same, but we all serve the same God.

DISCUSSION QUESTIONS

1. Have you ever been deterred from serving the Lord because of a personality conflict?

2. How did you handle it?

3. What could you have done differently?

Mary Magdalene - Tenacious Dedication

Jesus said to her, "Mary."

She turned toward him and cried out in
Aramaic, "Rabboni!" (which means "Teacher").

JOHN 20:16

MARY MAGDALENE IS MENTIONED only a few times in the New Testament narrative. However, in just a few words, we obtain a portrait of a courageous woman who dedicated her entire life to serving her Lord, Jesus Christ. Some modern authors have made false presumptions about Mary Magdalene that have cast a shadow on her character and put her integrity in doubt. While she may have been somewhat obscure as it relates to Christ's earthly ministry, she deserves to have her voice heard through the study of the passages that mention her by name. This will allow us to objectively reach a conclusion about her life and the ministry she had as a follower of Jesus.

The first time Mary Magdalene appears in the Bible is in the first few verses of Luke chapter 8. During Jesus' three-year ministry in Israel, he visited many places and we tend to think he traveled only with his twelve disciples. It's more likely there were many people, maybe even hundreds, with him. While Jesus obviously focused on training his disciples who were later called apostles, the gospels don't mention how many followers there really were. The large groups were highlighted more when a miracle was performed, thus demonstrating that more than just the disciples witnessed it. So, it seems logical to think there were many more than the disciples who accompanied Jesus and learned from him.

Several women are mentioned by name in the first three verses of Luke 8. They were women who had been healed of evil spirits and they accompanied Jesus on his journeys. One of these women was Mary Magdalene and it's clear that she served the Lord by financially supporting and participating in his ministry. The author of the gospel goes on to explain Mary Magdalene's condition before meeting Christ as having been possessed by seven demons.

It's difficult to imagine seven spirit beings roaming around in the mind and body of a person. Today's world would label Mary's infirmity as mental illness because having demons take over your mind and body would certainly make a person appear to be emotionally unstable. For Mary Magdalene the problem was so much more. She had no control whatsoever over any motor functions and her thought process would have been convoluted. It's reasonable to assume her emotional state changed often because seven beings vied for power over her body and mind. This must have been a torturous existence for her.

MARY MAGDALENE'S STORY

The story of Mary Magdalene's healing is not recorded in the gospels. However, there are other occasions in which the Lord rid individuals of demons. Once the evil spirits were gone, the change in the person was immediate and radical. All of a sudden, the afflicted person was in control of their own body again. A boy no longer threw himself into the fire. (Mark 9:22) A man put clothes on, sat with Jesus and had a conversation. (Mark 5:15) Mary Magdalene's conversion would have been similar.

Mary Magdalene must have been grateful to the point that she abandoned the life she had before and joined the disciples and others who traveled with Jesus from place to place. The change in

Mary Magdalene was so profound she followed him everywhere he went. Eventually, this would lead to the cross.

Mary Magdalene was saved from circumstances that consumed her life and dragged her down a path of destruction. The Savior stepped in and freed her from the bondage not just of demons, but sin as well. As a result, she became a disciple, a follower of Jesus. There was no going back for her. The life of Mary Magdalene became one of complete and utter devotion to Jesus and his ministry. She traveled with him. She served him. She supported him financially.

MARY MAGDALENE'S DEDICATION

When my children were not feeling well, they were usually only consoled if they were sitting in my lap with my arms wrapped around them. This was after a dose of acetaminophen to bring their fever down. They felt safe because they knew I cared. I would give them little kisses, and rock them gently. I would even hum a lullaby as they went back to sleep.

I was the one who got up in the middle of the night to hold a fevered child, bathe and soothe them. I would sit by their bed to keep vigil all night long or I would tuck them in with me. My relief was palpable when the fever broke. The day ahead would be a long one because I was tired. But the exhaustion was worth it when I saw my child interacting and playing.

The illustration above helps us to understand why women in general don't cut and run from trials. Mary Magdalene didn't either. She had to have been in Jerusalem during the last supper, Jesus' arrest, trial, and crucifixion. Of all the events listed, we know she was present at the worst, most gut-wrenching one—the crucifixion. We know because her presence is recorded in all four gospels. Her presence was so vital it had to be recorded according to each author's perspective.

Where were the men? They had scattered after Jesus' arrest. They made themselves scarce fearing they would be next to be taken and thrown in jail. The women? They were watching—maybe at a distance but watching. As gruesome a sight as it must have been, the women refused to run, turn their backs, and make Jesus endure the torture alone. Mary Magdalene was tenaciously resolved to stay with her Lord and Master.

Standing at the bedside of a loved one as they struggle with those last few pulls of oxygen is pure agony. I know because I experienced it with my husband, Doug, during the last twenty-four hours of his life. I stayed because I knew it was important to him. He didn't want to die alone. I didn't want him to die alone. And when the stillness came, the utter silence of death, the grief hit like a freight train. I left that bedside feeling like I was abandoning him. It didn't matter how many times I said to myself, "It's ok, he's not here anymore." I left with only half of myself because the other half was gone. It was excruciatingly painful, but I remained to the end and I would do it again.

We are women. Nurturers. We stay firm until we emerge on the other side—broken. When Jesus cried, "'It is finished,'" he gave himself over to death and Mary Magdalene was there. And she stayed.

Joseph of Arimathea requested Jesus' body. He would ensure the body was prepared and laid to rest in the Jewish tradition. Nicodemus came along to help and together, the two men hastily prepared Jesus' body with the fragrant spices, wrapped it in clean linen and laid the shell that had once been a living human being on a stone slab. A heavy stone sealed the body within in darkness. And Mary Magdalene was there.

It was a High Sabbath and the men didn't have much time to prepare the corpse. Perhaps they accomplished only some of the preparation because they had to bury Jesus before the sun set according to Jewish practice. They also had to hurry or they wouldn't return to their homes in time for the Seder. Mary Magdalene and the other women observed and planned. They would come back after the Sabbath and finish the preparation.

MARY MAGDALENE'S BLESSING

On the first day of the week, the day after the Sabbath, before the sun peeked over the horizon, Mary Magdalene was on her way to the tomb with the herbs and spices needed for Jesus's body.

Imagine her surprise when she arrived at the tomb only to discover the stone had been rolled away. It stood open. The guards lay flat out on the ground, unconscious, on either side of the entrance. Mary Magdalene poked her head in and saw the stone slab but no body. She looked around confused and disturbed. Who would take Jesus' body?

A man appeared and Mary Magdalene, thinking he was the gardener, asked, "'Do you know where they have put my Lord? Tell me and I will take His body away'" (John 20:15). Then the man whispered her name and Mary Magdalene realized it was Jesus! He was alive! Jesus had alluded to his resurrection on several occasions during his three years of ministry. It seems nobody listened. But now He was alive again! Mary Magdalene ran to tell the others what she had seen.

Mary Magdalene . . . a woman in anguish because evil spirits tormented her was healed by Jesus Christ. In her tenacious devotion to the man and his ministry, she accompanied him every step of the way. She followed him to the cross, to the grave and was the first to lay eyes on the resurrected Son of God. She was blessed.

DISCUSSION QUESTIONS

1. Mary's conversion was dramatic, to say the least, which could explain her devotion. What keeps those of us who were saved under less striking circumstances equally devoted to the Lord and His work?

2. Why do you think Jesus chose to reveal Himself to Mary first and not one of the disciples?

PART 5

Women Who Built a Church

Priscilla - Wise Scholar

*Greet Priscilla and Aquila, my co-workers in Christ
Jesus. They risked their lives for me. Not only I but all the
churches of the Gentiles are grateful to them.*

ROMANS 16:3-4

PRISCILLA IS FIRST MENTIONED in Acts 18 when she meets the
apostle Paul during his second missionary journey. She and her
husband being co-workers with Paul have been addressed in com-
mentaries, but there is little other information. Aquila and Priscilla
are mentioned six times in the New Testament. Four of those list
Priscilla first and this is what gives us the idea she was no small
figure in the early church.

PRISCILLA'S WORLD

By the time we get to the book of Acts, there has been a paradigm
shift in relation to how women were perceived. The Romans had
occupied Israel for many years. As a result, Roman culture was in-
fluencing centuries old beliefs and practices. Times were changing
and the establishment of the church on the Day of Pentecost, was
reaching farther and farther beyond Jerusalem. What was once
considered written in stone had been chiseled away and replaced
with more contemporary thought.

The Romans allowed their women to run businesses, hold office, divorce their husbands, and inherit property. Women were given freedoms they hadn't enjoyed before. However, some things still ran according to ancient, established practice. Many marriages were contracts between two families for political or monetary reasons and patriarchal in nature. In contrast, Greek and Jewish women did not enjoy these privileges. They were bound by the ancient traditions and laws that, in some cases, subjugated them to the status of servant in their own households. Priscilla found herself trapped between the two philosophies which, at the very least, made her life interesting.

Most of what we know of Priscilla is found in Acts 18. Paul had arrived in Corinth and met Aquila, a Roman Jew, and his wife Priscilla. The couple had been recently exiled from Italy by the Emperor Claudius. Paul, Aquila and Priscilla were all tentmakers and decided to start a tentmaking business together as a means of support for their daily needs.

The business relationship became a close friendship that would last many years. The three friends became partners in ministry. Their common love for the Word of God and burden to share the gospel with others drove them to the synagogue to "persuade Jews and Greeks." (Acts 18:4) Eventually a church was established in the city of Corinth.

This time period ended up being a pivotal moment for the Church. As with others, Paul's preaching in the synagogues was met with harsh resistance from the Jews. They didn't want to hear the gospel of Jesus Christ. The three missionaries were constantly looking over their shoulders wondering when they would be arrested, beaten, or thrown in jail. It happened often.

After so many threats from the Jewish population, Paul had had enough. He boldly declared before the Jews, "'From now on I will go to the Gentiles.'" Paul walked out of the synagogue and continued his missionary journey with Priscilla and Aquila in tow. They ended up in Ephesus where Aquila and Priscilla settled in for the long haul. The couple remained in Ephesus and planted a church while Paul went on to Caesarea then Antioch. It was during their time in Ephesus that Apollos visited their foundling church and was invited to preach. He was an eloquent young man and proficient with the Scriptures according to Acts 18:24.

PRISCILLA'S WISDOM

Apollos' preaching was accurate as it related to Jesus, his ministry, death, burial and resurrection, but when it came to baptism, he knew only about the baptism John the Baptist performed at the Jordan River. It appears Apollos had not been taught the doctrine of the Holy Spirit's baptism which is different. John's baptism by water was meant to demonstrate identity with Christ. Baptism by the Holy Spirit happens when a person comes to know the Lord in a spiritual and personal way. In other words, they begin a relationship with Jesus that lasts forever.

Apollos wasn't preaching heresy; he just didn't have all the information he needed to cover the topic well. Acts 18:26b states both Aquila and Priscilla took Apollos aside to explain what he was lacking in understanding. It was a team effort and apparently Priscilla and Aquila had a good ministry partnership because they shared the responsibility of gently correcting Apollos' understanding of the baptism by the Holy Spirit.

Think of the dynamic. Apollos was a biblical scholar from Alexandria in Egypt, a city known for being a center of learning. Aquila, as a husband, was head of the household. Some Bible translations list Aquila first, but when the passage is read in the original Greek language, Priscilla's name appears before Aquila's. This indicates she had an active role in the conversation. No matter how we look at it, Priscilla was a biblical scholar herself. She wouldn't be included in the account otherwise.

I feel very strongly believe that women must have a solid biblical and theological worldview. We were created and are meant to use our own minds and study skills to learn from God's Word. We are not to rely solely on others' teachings and interpretations. Our own study and understanding of the Scriptures are important to our spiritual growth and keep us from being led astray by the enemy. (Acts 17:11; Psalm 119:11)

PRISCILLA'S COURAGE

When we study Paul's missionary journeys, we learn he did not do all the church planting work alone. His partners in ministry were Barnabas, Silas, John Mark, Timothy, Priscilla and Aquila among others. It was a team effort and Priscilla played a large part in the establishment of the Church in Asia.

She and her husband also became Paul's friends. We know they were close because Paul mentions the couple with great affection in his greetings at the end of his letters. In his first letter to the Corinthian church, Paul sends greetings from Priscilla and Aquila. (Acts 16:19) Paul's second letter to Timothy contains a greeting to the couple who remained in Ephesus and were instrumental in the establishment of the church in that city. (2 Tim 4:19)

Priscilla and Aquila were in the habit of establishing a church from their own home no matter where that home was. This was the case in Ephesus according to 1 Corinthians 16:19. It was the case in Rome as well. They must have been allowed to return to Italy at some point because they ended up in Rome again. They didn't waste any time starting a church in the seat of the Roman Empire. (Rom 16:3–5)

The same passage in Romans mentions Priscilla and Aquila in a different circumstance. Paul stated they "risked their necks" (Romans 16:4) for him. He doesn't give details; Paul just spells it out. He's obviously grateful to them for saving his life and he understands the great risk they took to do so. It took a lot of courage to be willing to suffer severe consequences so Paul could be free to keep serving the Lord. Priscilla, alongside her husband, Aquila, proved themselves consistently faithful to the Lord's work. They also had a deep, lasting friendship with Paul.

Priscilla is a great example of a traveling missionary. She was obviously a major figure in establishing the church in Europe and Asia because she is mentioned so many times in relation to that type of ministry. She knew and understood the message of the Bible to the degree she was capable of teaching it to others, men included.

Her example for us today is still relevant. Priscilla, the woman, was a wife, a church planter, a biblical scholar, a theologian and a hard worker. Women can move forward in ministry with these same qualities and courage. It may even shape the world.

DISCUSSION QUESTIONS

1. Do you think you would be qualified to be a co-worker with Paul? Why or why not?

2. Would you have the courage to "risk your neck" for Paul?

Dorcas - Faithful Servant

Peter went with them, and when he arrived he was taken
upstairs to the room. All the widows stood around him,
crying and showing him the robes and other clothing that
Dorcas had made while she was still with them.

ACTS 9:39

WIDOWHOOD IS A STATE of being that nobody wants to experience. Besides losing a spouse, a widow realizes she has taken on previously shared responsibilities. Some of us find ourselves having to manage a budget and checking account. Car maintenance has become a necessary evil. Keeping a house from falling into disrepair is a constant worry. These are extra burdens we didn't anticipate. It's hard.

I've been a widow for seven and a half years. All the obligations mentioned above are true for me. My husband, Doug, took care of the cars. I even joked with him that I married him so he would do that. I knew nothing about cars. His father taught him about vehicle maintenance from a young age. Our house was always a joint project; we discussed everything. He managed the finances because, frankly, I had enough to do. On May 2, 2017, I became responsible for everything.

Since then, I've learned how to balance a budget, keep track of spending, and manage investments. My car's oil is changed every

5000 miles without fail. I watch the tire tread wear, the engine temperature and oil pressure. When the posts on my front porch showed signs of rotting, I called a trusted handyman who replaced them the next day. But I do it begrudgingly because I don't want to bear the weight of everything on my own.

Thankfully, there is a man in my church who helps me with projects that are beyond my knowledge. This spring he came over and sharpened the blades on my riding mower. He fixed the latch on the front door because I had installed it the wrong way. He's going to help me split firewood when I get the time to have it delivered. I appreciate this because, although I can do a lot of heavy lifting, there are certain tasks I would just prefer someone more qualified do. There are those in the church that have ministered to me in my need and I am eternally grateful.

The book of Acts narrates the account of one woman with two names who took it upon herself to encourage the widows in the city of Joppa. When we read the New Testament, the mixing of cultures between the Romans, Greeks and Jews gets confusing. This cultural blend caused many widows to become forgotten and destitute. However, the law of Moses was clear on the responsibility of the Jewish people to care for the widows in their midst. Enter Dorcas, also known as Tabitha. Like several New Testament people, she had a Jewish name and a Greek name. Tabitha was her Jewish name indicating she was a Jew by birth but she was more often called by her Greek name. Dorcas understood the widow's plight and took measures to decrease their suffering.

Dorcas was a gifted seamstress. She made robes and tunics and gave them to the widows to wear. Most of them didn't have the means to either buy ready-made garments or buy fabric to make their own. Dorcas' ministry was to buy the material and make clothing for the women. She obviously had an income to be able to do this and it's possible she also made clothing to sell and used the proceeds to buy what was needed for those neglected women.

Acts chapter 9 is commonly known to contain Paul's conversion on the road to Damascus. Interestingly enough, a couple other events happened around the same time. Peter healed two people from diverse backgrounds in cities that were a day's journey from each other. Peter had gone to Lydda to visit believers and encountered a paralyzed man. In the name of Jesus Christ, Peter healed the paralytic and "all the residents . . . saw him, and they turned to the Lord." (Acts 9:35)

DORCAS' INFLUENCE

Not far away, in the coastal town of Joppa, a disciple named Dorcas took ill and died. As was custom, the women washed her body in an upper room and prepared it for burial. News trickled in that Peter was in the nearby city of Lydda so the townspeople sent two men to bring him over to Joppa. The people were obviously distressed, and when they heard Peter was nearby, hope surged within their hearts that he might be able to heal Dorcas. So, they sent for the apostle. The two men, upon finding Peter, asked him urgently to return with them. Peter sensed their grief and rose quickly to go back with the men. When he arrived, they directed him to the upper room where Dorcas' body lay.

The widows were there weeping inconsolably while showing Peter the garments Dorcas had made for them. She was described as a disciple who was "full of good works and acts of charity." (Acts 9:36) It was probably noisy and chaotic in the cramped upper room where, in contrast, Dorcas' body lay still and silent. Peter sent everyone out of the room and in the quiet, he knelt and prayed. Then he called Dorcas by her Hebrew name and said, "'Tabitha, arise.'" (9:40)

Dorcas opened her eyes, sat up, then rose and went to the people waiting outside the chamber. Peter presented Dorcas to her loved ones who were overcome with joy. Their benefactor lived again! This was a powerful miracle Peter performed—so impressive that the news spread all over town. As a result, many believed and were saved.

Dorcas was one woman among many in Joppa. She could not have been the only seamstress, nor the only woman called a disciple of Jesus Christ. So, what was so special about Dorcas? If we look back at Mosaic law, we discover a few instructions given by God as it relates to women who have lost their husbands.

MOSAIC LAW

It shouldn't surprise us to learn widows were not forgotten by God. Deuteronomy 14:28–29 gives instructions on the tithe from the harvest. The Israelites were to bring one tenth of the produce of the earth every three years to store in the towns. What was in storage was only for the Levites/priests, the homeless, the orphans and the widows. The tithe (not a tax) was a reserve for the people who had no means of income or land to cultivate. They depended on the charity of others. The tithe the farmers brought to town was to feed those in need.

The Feast of Weeks, as explained in Deuteronomy 16, was a harvest festival in which the people gave thanks to the Lord for his provision. During the feast, the Israelites were to bring a freewill offering. The people bringing the offering decided how much they would give back to the Lord and this tribute was brought to the festival to share with the underprivileged and widows.

Deuteronomy 24:17–18 makes it clear the unfortunate, such as the orphans and widows were not to be exploited. If the widow owed money and gave her cloak as a pledge, she was to receive it back at the end of the day so she would not be cold that night as she slept. When the people beat the olive trees with sticks to loosen the ripe olives, they were to leave the ones still on the tree for the homeless, orphans and widows. In other words, the people were responsible to care for the unfortunate by feeding them and not taking advantage.

By remembering Mosaic law, the early church sought to take care of the destitute and especially the widows. When the church was established in Acts 2, care for the unfortunate was considered. There were so many without homes, parents or husbands, they were often cast aside and forgotten. This led to a miserable life of starvation, disease and death. Then there was the problem with the large number of widows being, the apostles had a difficult time keeping up with the study and preaching of the Word while taking caring for them. It caused so much distress that the twelve apostles gathered the disciples and chose seven men to perform the office of deacon, which means servant, and care for the widows. This relieved the apostles of a time-consuming task and they were able to spend more time in the Word and preparation of sermons.

DORCAS' SERVICE

Dorcas' ministry was important to the widows of Joppa and her loss left them with great uncertainty. God heard their despair and led Peter to bring her back from the dead. The widows benefitted from this, but the greater blessing was that many came to believe in the Lord. This was the true purpose of the miracle; to bring glory to God and to increase the church.

Ministry to widows is an important function of the church even today. Many are navigating uncharted waters and need assistance in practical ways. In Joppa, Dorcas made them clothes to wear. Like in the book of Ruth, gleaners would leave dropped wheat stalks or left olives on the tree for the poor and widows which provided with the means to survive. Today, the church will minister to widows in different ways. Someone may help the widow with setting up and balancing a budget. Another may take her car to have the oil changed. A church friend may even take the widow to lunch and ask her if she has immediate needs. These gifted saints will gladly do these things, not because they seek praise of their own. They seek to bring glory to God.

DISCUSSION QUESTION

1. Is there someone in the church who has been "widowed" we can come along side and encourage both materially and otherwise?

Lydia - Gracious Hostess

One of those listening was a woman from the city of Thyatira named Lydia, a dealer in purple cloth. She was a worshiper of God. The Lord opened her heart to respond to Paul's message.

ACTS 16:14

I LOVE TO ENTERTAIN and recently invited and friend and her mother for dinner. We had a great time enjoying food and conversation at the table. Later, we moved to the living room for dessert and more conversation. It's fun to invite people into my home, a relaxed atmosphere, and get to know them.

I also throw a great party—or so I've been told. When birthdays, anniversaries and holidays come around you can count on me to make the menu, decorate and plan games—with prizes. For my daughter's 16th birthday, we invited every girl in the school, a small American boarding school in Brazil. It was a sleepover and sixteen activities were planned for the night. The girls didn't make it past the tenth item on the list which was to watch a movie. They all fell asleep on the family room floor. I finished the last six items and went to bed. My daughter still considers it one of the best parties ever.

Inviting the pastor and his wife or one of the church families for dinner brings me great joy. It's an opportunity to watch people savoring the meal and building stronger bonds with the people of the church. I believe fellowship with other believers is essential to my own growth as a Christian. At the end of the evening everyone leaves with full bellies and encouraged hearts—mine included.

There will always be a need for people in the church to open their homes to visitors, sometimes on short notice. When we think about it, one person or family in the church is always willing to volunteer to host a missionary speaker. It doesn't matter if the hosts are involved in many church ministries, in home school activities, or even the community, they make a place to welcome a guest.

Hospitality is a gift. Some love to entertain and others who prefer to keep their home a private sanctuary. Some hosts take great care in preparing for visitors by deep cleaning guest bedrooms and bathrooms. Others will change the sheets on their child's bed, vacuum and dust a little. The "guest room" is ready. While some of us would think we must have a spotless home and an adequate room and bed for our guest, there are no hard and fast rules for hosting overnight visitors.

What's important to remember is that hospitality comes from the heart. The host's home may be a million-dollar mansion, but if there is no interaction with guests, are they really being hospitable? Or guests may find themselves in a bedroom the size of an ice cube, on a lower bunk with their suitcase shoved under the bed for lack of floor space. The host, however, has been available to talk and meet the guest's needs. In Acts 16 Paul and Silas encountered a woman who defined hospitality.

Paul was on his second missionary journey and had just received the call from the Lord to go to Macedonia. One of his first stops was the city of Philippi, a Roman colony in the region of Macedonia situated on a major trade route. Apparently, there was no synagogue in the city because on the Sabbath Paul and Silas went outside the city to the river. They had heard people gathered there for prayer. It was at the river's edge where they met Lydia.

LYDIA'S STORY

Lydia was a seller of purple dyed fabric. She came from the city of Thyatira. Tyrian purple was a dye extracted from sea snails and used to color fabric for royal households. Extracting and processing the dye was laborious and expensive. Only the very rich could afford the fabric and the seller of the dye was usually quite wealthy as well. It is very likely Lydia had homes in both Philippi and Thyatira, and she probably traveled between the two cities to sell her goods.

Lydia is described as a worshiper of God and was at the river for the prayer gathering when Paul and Silas arrived. Paul began to preach and Lydia listened with an open mind and heart. This led to her conversion in Jesus Christ. She became a Christian that day. It's as if she had been waiting for Paul to explain the gospel because she accepted it without hesitation. Paul's preaching also reached the servants of her household who were probably at the river with her because they were all baptized immediately after their conversion.

LYDIA'S MINISTRY

Afterward, Lydia invited Paul, Silas, and Luke, who was writing what would become known as the book of Acts, to her home. The men were hesitant, but Lydia urged them to go to her home and stay with her. She had never met them before that day. She had made no prior preparation for guests, but Lydia wanted them to come to her home. The men accepted her invitation.

Now, Lydia's home was probably spacious with many servants to meet the needs of guests on short notice. Her invitation, however, came from a desire to serve these travel weary men and give them a comfortable place to stay for a few days. She was serving the Lord by serving the missionaries.

During their stay in Philippi, Paul and Silas were thrown in jail for casting out demons from a young girl. The girl's masters had been using her and her ability to prophesy for their own financial gain. When the girl was relieved of the demons her masters' means of income disappeared. Indignant, the men registered a complaint with the city leadership. Paul and Silas were subsequently beaten and mocked publicly then thrown into prison. Around midnight, while the chained prisoners were praying and singing, an earthquake broke open the doors of the jailhouse and the manacles binding Paul and Silas. When the jailer awoke, he was sure the prisoners had all escaped—but they hadn't. The punishment for allowing the prisoners to escape was death. The jailer preferred suicide. As he pulled his sword from its sheath Paul cried out, "'Do not harm yourself, for we are all here'" (Acts 16:28). The jailer came to Christ that day.

Eventually, Paul and Silas were released and they went straight to Lydia's home where they knew they would be welcomed. They stayed long enough to fellowship with the believers and refresh themselves before departing for their next destination.

Lydia exercised hospitality with excellence. Paul and Silas' relationship with her was such that they were confident they could show up unannounced and be welcomed without hesitation. It is a rare thing to have friends like this, but when we do it is a great blessing. It's also a balm for the soul as it must have been for those men. Hospitality is a gift. It is also a condition of the heart; a means of ministering to those who are weary and need a place of comfort and rest.

DISCUSSION QUESTION

1. In what ways can we be more hospitable, both at church and in our homes?

Afterthoughts

"There is gold and abundance of costly stones, but the lips of knowledge are a precious jewel."

PROVERBS 20:15

THE JOURNEY TO WRITE this work began at least ten years ago and the women featured in it have taught me precious life lessons. An invitation to bring a study of a woman of the Bible to the women's group in the Casa Nova, BA church in Brazil was the catalyst. Afterward, whenever I was invited to bring a study, I would choose another woman. A pattern emerged and the title came about while pondering how these women's stories are relevant for today's world. Just as the Bible's relevance spans the entire history of the world, the part these women played is important for today.

My objective has been to help the reader achieve an understanding of God's view of and purpose for women. The wisdom we receive from the Word is more precious than any jewel as described in Proverbs 20:15. I, personally, have grown through the study of each woman. Their life lessons have been profound and have caused much reflection and meditation on my part. I've also gained the courage to engage in discussion with others when the names of these biblical women arise in conversation.

Gold, rubies, precious metals and stones are difficult to find and are not located within the territory of Israel. Most are brought from the far east or the African continent. Countries such as China,

Afghanistan and Australia contain mines where gold and rubies can be taken from the rock and sold to brokers. When the author of Proverbs uses the analogy of "lips of knowledge being a precious jewel," he is adding significant weight to his statement. The process to mine precious stones and metals is labor intensive, but it doesn't compare to the importance of knowledge of the Word of God.

When God tasked Moses and the Children of Israel with building a tabernacle in the desert he gave specific instructions as to which fabrics, skins, wood, precious metals and stones should be used. God called Moses at the burning bush and established that the Israelites would not leave Egypt empty-handed (Exodus 3:21-22). The assignment would seem impossible to accomplish were it not for the fact the Israelites had plundered the Egyptians before they left the country. The prophecy was fulfilled, and when it came time to put together the tabernacle, they had all the materials they needed. The structure would serve as the center of worship and sacrifice for the Children of Israel while they wandered in the desert. It was where God would dwell while he was with his people.

Moses asked for donations from those "'of a generous heart'" (Ex 35:5) which were used to build the tabernacle and make the priestly garments. While the tabernacle was being built, God separated Aaron and his sons to serve as priests. They, along with other Levites, would have the responsibility of overseeing everything that had to do with the tabernacle. The priests would wear special clothing made for the singular purpose of serving in the tabernacle. They were not worn at any other time. These garments were probably sewn by the women with great care using the finest fabrics and thread made of gold. They used several layers of linen, a soft, cool fabric, so the priests wouldn't sweat when they entered the tabernacle to perform their duties.

Then, precious stones were mounted on a breastplate fashioned of gold which the priest wore on his chest over the linen robes. There were four rows of three precious stones, each one different and representing a tribe of Israel named after the twelve sons of Jacob. One of the stones was a ruby which represented the tribe of Reuben, the firstborn of Jacob. The gold, linen, ruby, and other precious stones would have been part of the offering Moses collected.

Long after the Israelites conquered the land, Solomon built the temple in Jerusalem. The queen of Sheba (Ethiopia today) arrived for an extended visit. The queen brought many gifts to present to king Solomon which ranged from spices to wild animals to precious stones and metals. The primary purpose of her visit, though, was to see the man considered to be the wisest and wealthiest in the world. The queen asked Solomon many questions, all of which he answered to her satisfaction. The king then reciprocated by giving her many gifts to take back to Sheba with her. There has never been a regent with such great wisdom and wealth since Solomon.

Many years later, wise men came from the east to visit Jesus after his birth. They brought gifts of gold, frankincense, and myrrh. The gold would have come from their home region in the far east and was considered an acceptable gift for royalty. These men were astronomers who studied the constellations and the star that appeared one night in the sky signaling a significant event had taken place. It was one they had never seen before so the noblemen prepared to journey and discover its meaning. At the end of that trip, they encountered a young boy sitting on his mother's lap, presented their gifts, and went on their way. It's not unreasonable to conclude that news of a coming Messiah had reached these men which prompted them go and find out if it was true.

We understand today the significance of the gift of gold as a foreshadow of Christ's future reign over all the earth. The wise men were given the privilege of being first to acknowledge Christ's royal lineage. The gift of gold makes the illustration so much more significant when we realize these men had a glimpse of the future.

In all these examples the women seem to have taken a back seat role—even the queen of Sheba. They quietly made garments for the priests, they asked important questions so they might learn of the God of Israel and the famous wise king, and they quietly pondered the events around them as one watched her son become the ultimate sacrifice for sin. God saw and used the women to accomplish his purpose for them. He still sees and uses us today, and with that assurance, we are able to glean some valuable life lessons for our own spiritual growth—growth that can be passed from woman to woman and generation to generation. The wisdom we gain is truly more precious than the finest rubies and purest gold.

．．．．．．．．．．．．．

For Personal Use in
Preparation for the Chapter ahead

SARAH · MOTHER OF A NATION

Genesis 12:10–20

What do we learn about Sarah from this passage? _____

_____

_____

_____

_____

_____

What can we conjecture about Abraham and Sarah's relationship?

_____

_____

_____

_____

_____

Genesis 15

What are the details of the covenant God makes with Abraham?

_____

_____

_____

_____

_____

What is significant about the events in verses 17–19 in relation to the covenant? _____

_____

_____

_____

_____

_____

Genesis 16:1–6; Hebrews 11:11–12

What is revealed about Sarah's character in the Genesis 16 passage?

_____

_____

_____

_____

_____

_____

How does it contrast with what is said about her in Hebrews?

_____

_____

_____

_____

_____

_____

What should be our conclusion about Sarah? _____

_____

_____

_____

_____

_____

Genesis 17:15–27

Describe Abraham's reaction to the news that Sarah would bear him a son. _____

_____

_____

_____

_____

_____

Why is it significant that God will establish his covenant with Isaac and not Ishmael? _____

_____

_____

_____

_____

_____

Genesis 18:1–15

In what ways does Sarah's reaction to the visitors differ from that of Abraham's? _____

_____

_____

_____

_____

Genesis 21:1–7

Sarah's laughter is different now. What do you suppose happened between chapters 18 and 21 that turned her heart around?

_____

_____

_____

_____

_____

_____

REBEKAH - PLAYING FAVORITES

Genesis 24:10–28

Describe Rebekah in your own words based on what you read in the passage. _____

_____

_____

_____

_____

_____

Genesis 21:1–7

Genesis 24:29–61

We see a typical marriage contract negotiation taking place in these verses. Usually, the bride did not participate in this. What are the indications that Rebekah did, indeed, have a say in whether she would marry Isaac? _____

_____

_____

_____

_____

Genesis 21:1–7

Genesis 24:62–67; 25:19–28

Two very different sides of Rebekah are seen in these passages. What can we surmise of her character in 24:62–67?_____

_____

_____

_____

_____

Genesis 21:1–7

What about in 25:19–28? _____

_____

_____

_____

_____

_____

_____

Genesis 26:1–11

It says that Isaac loved Rebekah in 24:67. Yet we see a direct contrast to that in today's passage. What had changed in their relationship?

_____

_____

_____

_____

_____

_____

Genesis 27:1–29

It's obvious that Jacob is rather passive in these events doing everything his mother tells him. We know that Jacob was to receive the blessing from Isaac regardless. How do you think things would have been different if Rebekah had not interfered? _____

_____

_____

_____

_____

_____

_____

Genesis 28:1–9

Jacob receives specific instructions from Isaac as to what kind of woman he should marry. Why do you think Esau didn't receive the same being Isaac's favorite? _____

_____

_____

_____

_____

MIRIAM - FINISHING WELL

Hebrews 11:23–28

This passage is dedicated to the faith of Moses. However, verse 23 is referring Amram and Jochebed's faith. What can we learn from this? _____

_____

_____

_____

_____

_____

Exodus 1:8–22

Describe the mindset of the Egyptians. _____

_____

_____

_____

_____

Describe the mindset of the Hebrews. _____

_____

_____

_____

_____

Exodus 2:1–9

What do we learn about Miriam from this passage? _____

_____

_____

_____

_____

Exodus 15:19–21

How is Miriam described and what are her actions when the Hebrews witness the Egyptians demise? _____

_____

_____

_____

_____

_____

Numbers 12

Miriam and Aaron both spoke against Moses. Why do you think only Miriam was punished? _____

_____

_____

_____

_____

_____

Micah 6:4, 1 Chronicles 6:3

Miriam is mentioned in both passages along with her brothers. Why would the Lord include her? _____

_____

_____

_____

_____

_____

RAHAB - COURAGE UNDER FIRE

Joshua 2:1–7

The spies obviously didn't disguise themselves very well and when the king's men showed up at Rahab's home, they knew the spies were there. Rahab told a blatant lie to protect them. What do you think of this action? _____

_____
_____
_____
_____
_____
_____

Joshua 2:8–14

What is the attitude of the people of Jericho knowing that the Israelites are just across the river? _____

_____
_____
_____
_____
_____
_____

Joshua 2:15–21; James 2:24-26

What are the elements of the oath Rahab and the two spies make?

_____
_____
_____
_____
_____
_____

How did Rahab demonstrate her faith through works? _____

_____
_____
_____
_____
_____
_____

Joshua 2:22–24; Numbers 13:30–33

Describe the differences between the two spy missions. _____

_____
_____
_____
_____
_____
_____

Joshua 6:22–25

What happened to Rahab's family? _____

_____
_____
_____
_____
_____
_____

Matthew 1:1–6; Hebrews 11:31

There are four women mentioned in the Matthew passage, all of questionable character. Why do you think they are there? _____

_____
_____
_____
_____
_____
_____

DEBORAH - WISE WARRIOR

Judges 4:1–10

How is Deborah described in this passage? _____

_____
_____
_____
_____
_____
_____
_____

Judges 4:11–16

Barak appears to be a weak leader. What are the indications of this?

_____
_____
_____
_____
_____
_____
_____

Judges 4:17–24

Why would Jael give Sisera milk when he asked for water? _____

_____
_____
_____
_____
_____
_____
_____

Judges 5:1–9

This song of praise begins with a tribute to the Lord's power then Deborah describes the condition of Israel before she became judge. What was it? _____

_____

_____

_____

_____

_____

Judges 5:10–18

These verses list which clans joined in the battle and which didn't. Which clans made up the army that conquered Sisera? _____

_____

_____

_____

_____

_____

Judges 5:19–31

Which verses describe the fulfillment of the prophecy Deborah made? _____

_____

_____

_____

_____

_____

RUTH AND NAOMI - PICTURE OF REDEMPTION

Ruth 1:1–7

These verses set the stage for the rest of the narrative. What are the key events? _____

_____

_____

_____

_____

Ruth 1:8–14

Naomi is determined to return to Israel alone. Ruth determines to go with her. What makes this a risky move? _____

_____

_____

_____

_____

Ruth 1:15–22

What are the elements of Ruth's declaration of faith? _____

_____

_____

_____

_____

What is Naomi's attitude throughout the chapter? _____

_____

_____

_____

_____

Ruth 2

In what ways do we see God's hand in the events of Ruth's first day in the barley field? _____

_____

_____

_____

_____

_____

_____

Ruth 3

What risks was Ruth taking by going to the threshing floor at night? _____

_____

_____

_____

_____

_____

Ruth 4
What are the climax and resolution of the story? _____

_____

_____

_____

_____

_____

Who comes back into the spotlight at the end of the book? _____

_____

_____

_____

_____

_____

HANNAH - HOPE IN ADVERSITY

1 Samuel 1:1–2

The name Hannah means grace, charm, favor, popularity. How is this name ironic based on what we read in these verses? _____

_____

_____

_____

_____

1 Samuel 1:3–8

Describe Hannah's situation. _____

_____

_____

_____

_____

Does it appear Elkanah may have been a little oblivious to her feelings? _____

_____

_____

_____

_____

1 Samuel 1:9–11, Numbers 6:1–8

Explain the level of dedication Hannah intended for her son.

_____

_____

_____

_____

1 Samuel 1:12–18

Speculate. Why do you think Eli would so completely misinterpret what Hannah was doing? _____

_____

_____

_____

_____

_____

1 Samuel 1:19–20

The name Samuel means "asked of God". What does this tell us of Hannah's character? _____

_____

_____

_____

_____

_____

1 Samuel 1:21–28

What is the wisdom in Hannah waiting until Samuel was weaned (about three years old) before she took him to the Tabernacle to live with Eli? _____

_____

_____

_____

_____

_____

MARY - MOTHER OF JESUS

Luke 1:26–33

Gabriel cites several Old Testament prophecies in these verses. What are they and where are they found? _____

_____

_____

_____

_____

_____

_____

Luke 1:34–38

Why did Gabriel mention Elizabeth's pregnancy to Mary? _____

_____

_____

_____

_____

_____

Luke 1:39–45

The word blessed is used three times in this passage. The first two mean "divine favor" and the third "pertaining to being happy." Both are important to understanding the context of the passage. How? _____

_____

_____

_____

_____

_____

_____

Luke 1:46–55; 1 Samuel 2:1–10

Both passages are songs of praise after a significant encounter with God's power. How are they similar? _____

_____

_____

_____

_____

_____

Luke 1:46–55

Mary cites several Old Testament passages. What does this tell us of her? _____

_____

_____

_____

_____

_____

Luke 1:54–56

Mary is making a declaration of the Lord's faithfulness. What is it specifically? _____

_____

_____

_____

_____

_____

MARY AND MARTHA - COMPLETE OPPOSITES/ FAITHFUL SERVANTS

Luke 10:38–42

Describe Martha's frame of mind in this incident. _____

_____

_____

_____

_____

_____

_____

John 11:1–16

Verse 5 says Jesus loved Mary, Martha and Lazarus. The next verse says he stayed two more days where he was. Does this look like the actions of a person who truly loves? Explain. _____

_____

_____

_____

_____

_____

_____

John 11:17–27

Martha's actions are typical of her personality type and in this case, it allows for her to have a conversation with Jesus. What does this tell us of her knowledge and commitment? _____

_____

_____

_____

_____

_____

_____

John 11:28–37

Mary only goes to Jesus when he calls her. What is her response?

_____

_____

_____

_____

_____

_____

John 11:38–44

Martha is rebuked again by Jesus. What is the reason this time?

_____

_____

_____

_____

_____

_____

John 12:1–7

Jesus is back in Bethany just before the Passover and Martha is serving. Why is she not rebuked this time? _____

_____

_____

_____

_____

_____

What do Mary's actions tell us about her? _____

_____

_____

_____

_____

_____

MARY MAGDALENE - TENACIOUS DEDICATION

Luke 8:1–3

Luke mentions three women by name. What is significant about them? _____

_____

_____

_____

_____

_____

Matthew 27:55–61

Mary Magdalene is mentioned again by name. What was her role during and after the crucifixion? _____

_____

_____

_____

_____

_____

Mark 15:40–47; Luke 23:27, 44–56

What were the women doing in these passages? _____

_____

_____

_____

_____

_____

John 19:23–42

Several prophecies are fulfilled in this passage. What are they?

Psalm 22:16–18 _____

_____

Luke 2:35 _____

_____

Exodus 12:46; Numbers 9:12; Psalm 34:20 _____

_____

Zechariah 12:10; Isaiah 53:5 _____

_____

Matthew 28:1–10; Mark 16:1–11

Describe the events of the resurrection. _____

_____

_____

_____

_____

_____

_____

Luke 24:1–12; John 20: 1–18

Describe the gamut of emotions Mary must have been feeling and
what indicates each one. _____

_____

_____

_____

_____

_____

_____

PRISCILLA · WISE SCHOLAR

Acts 18:1–17

What did Aquila and Priscilla have in common with Paul?_____
_____
_____
_____
_____
_____

Acts 18:18–23

What would be the purpose of Priscilla and Aquila accompanying Paul to Ephesus and then staying behind while he went to Jerusalem?
_____
_____
_____
_____
_____

Acts 18:24–28

On what doctrinal aspect did Priscilla and Aquila need to instruct Apollos? _____
_____
_____
_____
_____
_____

Who took the primary teaching role? _____
_____
_____
_____
_____

Romans 16:3–5

What is the level of friendship between Paul and Priscilla and Aquila? _____

_____

_____

_____

_____

_____

_____

1 Corinthians 16:19–23

Where are Aquila and Priscilla now? _____

_____

_____

_____

_____

_____

2 Timothy 4:9–22

This is one of four instances in which Priscilla's name is mentioned before Aquila's. Why would that be? Look within the context of all the passages read this week. _____

_____

_____

_____

_____

_____

DORCAS - FAITHFUL SERVANT

Acts 9:32–35

What else happened besides Peter curing Aeneas? _____

_____

_____

_____

_____

_____

Acts 9:36–38

How is Dorcas described in these verses and how is it different from the description of Aeneas? _____

_____

_____

_____

_____

_____

Acts 9:39–43

This occasion of "bringing back to life" is reminiscent of several others in the Scriptures. Name one of them. _____

_____

_____

_____

_____

_____

_____

LYDIA - GRACIOUS HOSTESS

Acts 16:11–15

What can we learn of Lydia from this passage? _____

_____

_____

_____

_____

Acts 16:25–34

What was the incident in the Philippian jail that brought the guard to his knees? _____

_____

_____

_____

_____

Acts 16:35–40

After his release, Paul makes it a point to visit Lydia again. Why do you think that is? _____

_____

_____

_____

_____

Bibliography

Clark, Mauro. (2011). Quem é Ele, Afinal? Editora Batista Regular, São Paulo, SP.

https://www.compellingtruth.org/womens-rights.html

https://www.gotquestions.org/Bible-sexism.html

https://griekse-les.nl/women-and-their-role-in-ancient-greece-and-rome/

https://www.gty.org/library/articles/A265/the-biblical-portrait-of-women-setting-the-record-straight

http://www.religioustolerance.org/cfe_bibl.htm

https://www.oed.com/search/dictionary/?scope=Entries&q=disciple

www.ingramcontent.com/pod-product-compliance
Lightning Source LLC
Chambersburg PA
CBHW070444090426
42735CB00012B/2457